THE DISCIPLINE OF GRACE

God's Role and Our Role in the Pursuit of Holiness

by Jerry Bridges

The Navigators is an international Christian organization. Jesus Christ gave His followers the Great Commission to go and make disciples (Matthew 28:19). The aim of The Navigators is to help fulfill that commission by multiplying laborers for Christ in every nation.

NavPress is the publishing ministry of The Navigators. NavPress publications are tools to help Christians grow. Although publications alone cannot make disciples or change lives, they can help believers learn biblical discipleship, and apply what they learn to their lives and ministries.

©1994 by Jerry Bridges
All rights reserved. No part of this publication may be reproduced in any form without written permission from NavPress, P. O. Box 35001, Colorado Springs, CO 80935.
Library of Congress Catalog Card Number: 94-31041
ISBN 08910-98836

Cover photograph: Copyright © 1994 Teruto Shintani/ Mon-Trésor/Panoramic Images, Chicago, all rights reserved

Some of the anecdotal illustrations in this book are true to life and are included with the permission of the persons involved. All other illustrations are composites of real situations, and any resemblance to people living or dead is coincidental.

Unless otherwise identified, all Scripture quotations in this publication are taken from the *HOLY BIBLE: NEW INTERNATIONAL VERSION* ® (NIV®). Copyright © 1973, 1978, 1984 by International Bible Society. Used by permission of Zondervan Publishing House. All rights reserved. Other versions used include: the *New American Standard Bible* (NASB), © The Lockman Foundation 1960, 1962, 1963, 1968, 1971, 1972, 1973, 1975, 1977; and the *King James Version* (KJV).

Bridges, Jerry.
     The discipline of grace : God's role and our role in the pursuit of holiness / Jerry Bridges.
          p.   cm.
     Includes bibliographical references.
     ISBN 0-89109-883-6
     1. Holiness—Christianity. 2. Grace (Theology)
3. Discipline—Religious aspects—Christianity. 4. Conduct of life.
I. Title.
BT767.B826 1994
234'.8—dc20   94-31041
                                                                                        CIP

Printed in the United States of America

1 2 3 4 5 6 7 8 9 10 11 12 13 14 15 16 17 18 19 20 21 22 / 99 98 97 96 95 94

CONTENTS

To my dear wife
Jane,
whom God gave to me
in the "afternoon" of my life

And to
Grace Peterson,
a "senior saint" who has been
a faithful prayer supporter
for many years

And most of all
"To him who loves us and has freed us
from our sins by his blood—
to him be glory and power
for ever and ever! Amen."
—Revelation 1:6

PREFACE

Shortly after my book *The Pursuit of Holiness* was published in 1978, I was invited to give a series of ten lectures on that subject at a church in our city. One night I titled my lecture "The Chapter I Wish I Had Written." The nature of that message was that the pursuit of holiness must be motivated by an ever-increasing understanding of the grace of God; else it can become oppressive and joyless.

The study and reflection that went into that lecture started me down the path of further study on the grace of God, culminating in a later book, *Transforming Grace*. As I sought to relate the biblical principle of living by grace to the equally biblical principle of personal discipline, I realized that it would be helpful to bring these two truths together in one book. That is the purpose of this volume.

A publisher's deadline is both a slave master and a friend. It is a slave master in that it keeps my "nose to the grindstone" when there are so many other things calling, even screaming, for my attention (such as my garage, which desperately needs my attention). The deadline is a friend, however, in that it forces me to say, "Enough is enough." It seems I am continually thinking of more things I want to say, but there comes a time when I must turn over a finished manuscript to the editor and trust that the Holy Spirit has prompted me to say all that needs to be said.

One of the more difficult aspects for me of writing a book about grace and holiness is the continual need for self-examination, lest I become like the teachers of the law and the Pharisees of whom Jesus said, "'They do not practice

7

what they preach'" (Matthew 23:3). The self-examination is often painful, and I have to confess that I struggle to apply much of what I have written in this book. That is why you will find a continual emphasis on the gospel of God's grace in Jesus Christ. It is only the gospel that keeps me pursuing holiness, and it is only the assurance of His grace in Christ that gives me the courage to pass on what I have learned and am still learning.

One of my life verses, which gives both direction and motivation, is Ephesians 3:8: "Although I am less than the least of all God's people, this grace was given me: to preach to the Gentiles the unsearchable riches of Christ." It is in that spirit that I submit this book to you.

One of the joys of writing a preface is the opportunity to express appreciation to those who have helped in one way or another in the writing of a book. To that end I must first of all acknowledge the giants who have gone before me and from whose writings I have profited so much. I think particularly of the Puritan theologian John Owen, who, in his writings, has taught me so much about the pursuit of holiness. Next among those who have gone before would be the nineteenth-century Scottish theologian George Smeaton, through whom I have come to a richer understanding of the gospel.

I also owe a debt of gratitude to my friend Dr. Jack Miller, from whom I acquired the expression "Preach the gospel to yourself every day." I had been doing that, somewhat out of necessity, for several years, but Dr. Miller helped bring that concept into sharper focus and more conscious application for me.

My friend Don Simpson read the manuscript and gave me valuable feedback and suggestions. This is the third time Don has helped me by reading a manuscript, and he has been a faithful friend. Steve Webb, my editor at NavPress, has also given valuable suggestions and encouragement. Many of my friends across the country responded to an "SOS" for prayer support when I was about halfway through the book and so discouraged I was ready to give it up. You know who you are, so thank you so very, very much.

Sue Zeug, my assistant, typed the manuscript, including numerous revisions, since I am still trying to come into the computer age. My wife, Jane, has again encouraged me by her prayers and patience during the time I have devoted my attention to this book.

Most of all I am grateful to God, who has given me the privilege of ministering to others through the printed page. I am certainly an unworthy servant, and it is, again, only by His grace that I have this ministry.

1

How Good Is Good Enough?

"Why do you call me good?" Jesus answered.
"No one is good—except God alone."
Mark 10:18

AS I WAS SITTING in the doctor's waiting room one day, my eye was drawn to a remarkable picture of a man being sculpted. The sculpture was complete down to about midthigh, and the finished work showed a very robust and muscular man with the kind of physique all men would like to have. The striking thing about the picture, however, was that the artist had put the hammer and chisel in the hands of the man being sculpted.

I was fascinated by the picture and wondered what message the artist was trying to convey. Perhaps he was trying to paint a picture of the so-called self-made man. As I studied the picture, however, I marveled at how it did depict so well the way many Christians try to live the Christian life. We try to change ourselves. We take what we think are the tools of spiritual transformation into our own hands and try to sculpt ourselves into robust Christlike specimens. But spiritual transformation is primarily the work of the Holy Spirit. He is the Master Sculptor.

However, we must not press this analogy too far. The picture was of a block of marble being sculpted into a man. Both the original piece of marble and the finished product were inert, lifeless forms. That is not true in our case. We are endowed with reason, emotions, and a will, all of which were renewed at the time we trusted Christ for salvation, and which the Holy Spirit works through as He involves us in the transforming process.

The Holy Spirit's work in transforming us more and more into the likeness of Christ is called sanctification. Our involvement and cooperation with Him in His work is what I call the pursuit of holiness. That expression is not original with me. Rather, it is taken from Hebrews 12:14—"Make every effort [literally: pursue] . . . to be holy; without holiness no one will see the Lord."

The pursuit of holiness requires sustained and vigorous effort. It allows for no indolence, no lethargy, no halfhearted commitment, and no laissez faire attitude toward even the smallest sins. In short, it demands the highest priority in the life of a Christian, because to be holy is to be like Christ— God's goal for every Christian.

The word *pursue* in this context means to strive to gain or accomplish. Note the strong verb *strive*. As we have already seen, the Greek word for pursue is translated "make every effort" in Hebrews 12:14. In Philippians 3:12-14, it is translated "press on." The most common use of it in the New Testament, however, is translated "persecute" and carries the common meaning of that word—to track down in order to harm or destroy. It is a very vigorous word.

At the same time, however, the pursuit of holiness must be anchored in the grace of God; otherwise it is doomed to failure. That statement probably strikes many people as strange. A lot of Christians seem to think that the grace of God and the vigorous pursuit of holiness are antithetical— that is, in direct and unequivocal opposition to one another.

To some, the pursuit of holiness sounds like legalism and manmade rules. To others, an emphasis on grace seems to open the door to irresponsible, sinful behavior based on the notion that God's unconditional love means we are free to sin as we please.

Some years ago I wrote a book titled *The Pursuit of Holiness*[1] in which I strongly emphasized our responsibility for holiness as opposed to the concept of just turning it all over to God. Thirteen years later I wrote another book, *Transforming Grace*,[2] in which I urged believers to learn to live by grace, not by performance. After *Transforming Grace* was published, many people asked me how it related to *The Pursuit of Holiness*. The question always seemed to carry the suggestion that grace and the pursuit of holiness are incompatible. One lady even went so far as to wonder how the same person who wrote the book on holiness could possibly have written a book on grace.

Grace and the personal discipline required to pursue holiness, however, are not opposed to one another. In fact, they go hand in hand. An understanding of how grace and personal, vigorous effort work together is essential for a lifelong pursuit of holiness. Yet many believers do not understand what it means to live by grace in their daily lives, and they certainly don't understand the relationship of grace to personal discipline.

Consider two radically different days in your own life. The first one is a good day spiritually for you. You get up promptly when your alarm goes off and have a refreshing and profitable quiet time as you read your Bible and pray. Your plans for the day generally fall into place, and you somehow sense the presence of God with you. To top it off, you unexpectedly have an opportunity to share the gospel with someone who is truly searching. As you talk with the person, you silently pray for the Holy Spirit to help you and to also work in your friend's heart.

The second day is just the opposite. You don't arise at the first ring of your alarm. Instead, you shut it off and go back to sleep. When you finally awaken, it's too late to have a quiet time. You hurriedly gulp down some breakfast and rush off to the day's activities. You feel guilty about over-sleeping and missing your quiet time, and things just generally go wrong all day. You become more and more irritable as the day wears on, and you certainly don't sense God's presence in your life. That evening, however, you quite unexpectedly have an opportunity to share the gospel with someone who is really interested in receiving Christ as Savior.

Would you enter those two witnessing opportunities with a different degree of confidence? Would you be less confident on the bad day than on the good day? Would you find it difficult to believe that God would bless you and use you in the midst of a rather bad spiritual day?

If you answered yes to those questions, you have lots of company among believers. I've described these two scenarios to a number of audiences and asked, "Would you respond differently?" Invariably, about 80 percent indicate that they would. They would be less confident of God's blessing while sharing Christ at the end of a bad day than they would after a good one. Is such thinking justified? Does God work that way? The answer to both questions is no, because God's blessing does not depend on our performance.

Why then do we think this way? It is because we do believe that God's blessing on our lives is somehow conditioned upon our spiritual performance. If we've performed well and had a "good" day, we assume we are in a position for God to bless us. Oh, we know God's blessings come to us through Christ, but we also have this vague but very real notion that they are also conditioned on our behavior. A friend of mine used to think, *If I do certain things, then I can get God to come through for me.*

Such thinking is even stronger when we've had a "bad" day. There is virtually no doubt in our minds that we have forfeited God's favor for some period of time, most likely until the next day. I've asked people why they think God would probably not use them to share the gospel with someone on a "bad" day. A typical reply is, "I wouldn't be worthy," or "I wouldn't be good enough."

Such a reply reveals an all-too-common misconception of the Christian life: the thinking that, although we are saved by grace, we earn or forfeit God's blessings in our daily lives by our performance.

A BAD DAY

So what should we do when we've had a "bad" day spiritually, when it seems we've done everything wrong and are feeling very guilty? We must go back to the cross and see Jesus there bearing our sins in His own body (1 Peter 2:24). We must by faith appropriate for ourselves the blood of Christ that will cleanse our guilty consciences (see Hebrews 9:14).

For example, in the bad-day scenario I've described, we might pray to God something like the following:

Father, I have sinned against You. I've been negligent in the spiritual disciplines that I know are necessary and helpful for my spiritual growth. I've been irritable and impatient toward those around me. I've allowed resentful and unkind thoughts to lodge in my mind. I repent of these sins and claim Your forgiveness.

You have said You justify the wicked (Romans 4:5). Father, in view of my sins today, I acknowledge that in myself I am wicked. In fact, my problem is not merely the sins I've committed, some of which I may not even be aware of, but the fact that my heart is sinful. These sins I am so painfully conscious of now are merely the expressions of my sinful heart.

But despite my sins and my sinfulness, You have said, "There is now no condemnation for those who are in Christ Jesus" (Romans 8:1). Given my acute awareness of my sin just now, that seems to be an incredible statement. How can I be without condemnation when I have so flagrantly and willfully sinned against You today?

O Father, I know it is because Jesus bore the sins

I've committed today in His body on the cross. He suffered the punishment I deserve, so that I might experience the blessings He deserved. So I come to You, dear Father, and in Jesus' name I ask You to enable me to effectively share the gospel with this friend just now.

You can readily see by the spirit of humility expressed in that prayer that I am not proposing a cavalier attitude toward sin. Rather, I am saying that God's grace through Christ is greater than our sin, even on our worst days. To experience that grace, however, we must lay hold of it by faith in Christ and His death on our behalf. Now, your particular prayer may not be as long as the one I've written. The issue is not how long your prayer is; it is the attitude of your heart. Do the sentiments expressed in that prayer reflect your heart attitude? I have read that every time the great nineteenth-century preacher Charles Spurgeon stepped into the pulpit, he did so with the silent prayer, "God be merciful to me a sinner" (Luke 18:13, KJV). Spurgeon's one-sentence prayer captures all I've expressed in four paragraphs.

You can pray a prayer like this whenever you are acutely aware of your need of God's intervening grace and at the same time are painfully aware of your total undeservedness of that grace. In fact, we obviously should not wait until we have a need for God to bless us. We should pray such a prayer of repentance and faith just to have our consciences cleansed from all sin and to walk in fellowship with God.

A GOOD DAY
Now, let's go back to the good-day scenario, the day when your spiritual disciplines are all in place and you are reasonably satisfied with your Christian performance. Have you thereby earned God's blessing that day? Will God be pleased to bless you because you've been good? You are

probably thinking, *Well, when you put it like that, the answer is no. But doesn't God only work through clean vessels?* To which I reply, "Let's assume that is true. How good then do you have to be to be a clean vessel? *How good is good enough?*"

When one of the Pharisees asked Jesus, "Teacher, which is the greatest commandment in the Law?" Jesus replied: "'Love the Lord your God with all your heart and with all your soul and with all your mind.' This is the first and greatest commandment. And the second is like it: 'Love your neighbor as yourself'" (Matthew 22:37-39).

Using Jesus' response to the Pharisee as a standard, how good has your good day been? Have you perfectly kept those two commandments? If not, does God grade on a curve? Is 90 percent a passing grade with God? We know the answers to those questions, don't we? We know that Jesus said, "Be perfect, therefore, as your heavenly Father is perfect" (Matthew 5:48). And we remember that James wrote, "For whoever keeps the whole law and yet stumbles at just one point is guilty of breaking all of it" (James 2:10).

The point of this good-day–bad-day comparison is this: Regardless of our performance, we are always dependent on God's grace, His undeserved favor to those who deserve His wrath. Some days we may be more acutely conscious of our sinfulness and hence more aware of our need of His grace, but there is never a day when we can stand before Him on our own two feet of performance, when we are worthy enough to deserve His blessing.

At the same time, the good news of the gospel is that God's grace is available on our worst days. That is true because Christ Jesus fully satisfied the claims of God's justice and fully paid the penalty of a broken law when He died on the cross in our place. Because of that the Apostle Paul could write, "He forgave us all our sins" (Colossians 2:13).

Does the fact that God has forgiven us all our sins mean that He no longer cares whether we obey or disobey? Not at all. The Scripture speaks of our grieving the Holy Spirit through our sins (Ephesians 4:30). And Paul prayed that we "may please [God] in every way" (Colossians 1:10). We grieve God and we please God. Clearly, He cares about our conduct and will discipline us when we refuse to repent of conscious sin. But God is no longer our Judge. Through Christ He is now our heavenly Father who disciplines us only out of love and only for our good.

If God's blessings were dependent on our performance, they would be meager indeed. Even our best works are shot through with sin—with varying degrees of impure motives and lots of imperfect performance. We are always, to some degree, looking out for ourselves, guarding our flanks, protecting our egos. It is because we do not realize the utter depravity of the principle of sin that remains in us and stains everything we do, that we entertain any notion of earning God's blessings through our obedience. And it is because we do not fully grasp the fact that Jesus paid the penalty for *all* our sins that we despair of God's blessing when we have failed to live up to even our own desires to live a life that is pleasing to God.

Here is an important spiritual principle that sums up what I've said thus far:

> Your worst days are never so bad that you are beyond the *reach* of God's grace. And your best days are never so good that you are beyond the *need* of God's grace.

Every day of our Christian experience should be a day of relating to God on the basis of His grace alone. We are not only saved by grace, but we also live by grace every day. This grace comes through Christ, "through whom we have gained access by faith into this grace in which we now *stand*" (Romans 5:2, emphasis added).

A significant part of the Mosaic Law was the promise of blessings for obedience and curses for disobedience (see Deuteronomy 28, especially verses 1-2 and 15). Some Christians live as if that principle applies to them today. But Paul said that "the law was put in charge to lead us to Christ that we might be justified by faith" (Galatians 3:24). Christ has already borne the curses for our disobedience and earned for us the blessings of obedience. As a result we are now to look to Christ alone—not Christ plus our performance—for God's blessings in our lives. We are saved by grace and we are to live by grace alone.

When we pray to God for His blessing, He does not examine our performance to see if we are worthy. Rather, He looks to see if we are trusting in the merit of His Son as our only hope for securing His blessing. To repeat: We are saved by grace, and we are to live by grace every day of our Christian lives.

If it is true that our relationship with God is based on His grace instead of our performance, why then are we so prone to fall into the good-day–bad-day type of thinking? It is because we have relegated the gospel to the unbeliever.

A LIFETIME MESSAGE

Consider a simple time line of your life as shown by the following illustration. It has only three points of time: your birth, your death, and the day of your salvation. Regardless of your age when you trusted Christ, the Cross divides your whole life into two periods: you as an unbeliever and you as a believer.

With this time line in mind, what one word describes the Bible message you most needed to hear as an unbeliever? I suggest that word is the *gospel*. It is the gospel that is the power of God for salvation (Romans 1:16). We need to hear that Jesus died for sinners and that if we come to Him in faith, we will receive the forgiveness of our sins and the gift of eternal life. The message may be "packaged" in any number of ways, but it must always be the gospel. That is what

we need to hear and respond to as unbelievers. Now the
time line of your life looks like this:

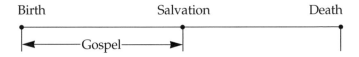

What one word describes the message we most need to
hear as believers? I get a lot of different answers to that question, but most of them can be summed up with one word,
discipleship. After all, Jesus did say, "Go and make disciples
of all nations" (Matthew 28:19). As believers we are continually challenged with the demands and duties of discipleship. These demands and duties include such things as the
spiritual disciplines (quiet time, Bible study, prayer, worship, church attendance, etc.); obedience to God's moral will
set forth in the Bible or, as I call it, the pursuit of holiness;
and service or ministry for the Kingdom of God. Almost
everything we need to do as believers is probably included
in the three words *disciplines*, *holiness*, and *service*.

So now our time line looks like this:

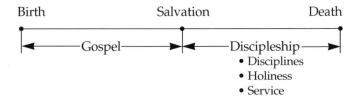

This time line illustrates how we tend to view the
Christian life—the gospel for unbelievers and the duties of discipleship for believers. I don't question our emphasis on discipleship. As I have already observed, Jesus did say, "Go and
make disciples." If anything, we need more challenge and
instruction on this threefold emphasis of disciplines, holiness, and service. But there is something more basic than
discipleship, something that actually provides the necessary
atmosphere in which discipleship can be practiced. The one

word that describes what we must continue to hear is *gospel*.

We need to continue to hear the gospel every day of our Christian lives. Only a continuous reminder of the gospel of God's grace through Christ will keep us from falling into good-day–bad-day thinking, wherein we think our daily relationship with God is based on how good we've been.

It is only the joy of hearing the gospel and being reminded that our sins are forgiven in Christ that will keep the demands of discipleship from becoming drudgery. It is only gratitude and love to God that comes from knowing that He no longer counts our sins against us (Romans 4:8) that provides the proper motive for responding to the claims of discipleship.

SELF-RIGHTEOUSNESS AND GUILT

We must remember, however, that the gospel is for sinners. Jesus said, "I have not come to call the righteous, but sinners to repentance" (Luke 5:32). The gospel is meaningful for us only to the extent that we realize and acknowledge that we are still sinful. Although we are new creations in Christ, we still sin every day in thought, word, and deed, and perhaps even more importantly, in motives. To benefit from the gospel every day, then, we must acknowledge that we are still sinners.

Without a continual reminder of the good news of the gospel, we can easily fall into one of two errors. The first is to focus on our external performance and become proud like the Pharisees. We may then begin to look down our spiritual noses at others who are not as disciplined, obedient, and committed as we are and in a very subtle way begin to feel spiritually superior to them.

The second error is the exact opposite of the first. It is the feeling of guilt. We have been exposed to the disciplines of the Christian life, to obedience, and to service, and in our hearts we have responded to those challenges. We haven't, however, been as successful as others around us appear to be. Or we find ourselves dealing with some of the sins of the heart such as anger, resentment, covetousness, and a judgmental attitude. Perhaps we struggle with impure thoughts or impatience, or a lack of faith and trust in God. Because we have put the gospel on the shelf as far as our own lives are concerned, we struggle with a sense of failure and guilt. We believe God is displeased with us, and we certainly wouldn't expect His blessing on our lives. After all, we don't deserve His favor.

Because we are focusing on our performance, we forget the meaning of grace: God's unmerited favor to those who deserve only His wrath. Pharisee-type believers unconsciously think they have earned God's blessing through their behavior. Guilt-laden believers are quite sure they have forfeited God's blessing through their lack of discipline or their disobedience. Both have forgotten the meaning of grace because they have moved away from the gospel and have slipped into a performance relationship with God.

Most of us probably entertain either of these attitudes on different days. On a good day, as we perceive it, we tend toward self-righteous Pharisaism. On a not-so-good day we allow ourselves to wallow in a sense of failure and guilt. In fact, it may be more than not-so-good days—it may be weeks or months. But whether it is weeks or days, the problem is the same. We have moved away from the gospel of God's grace and have begun to try to relate to God directly on the basis of our performance rather than through Christ.

God never intended that we relate to Him directly. Our own performance is never good enough to be acceptable to Him. The only way we can relate to God is through the blood and righteousness of Jesus Christ. It is only the blood of Jesus that will cleanse us from a guilty conscience and give us the confidence to enter into the presence of God (Hebrews 10:19-21).

The gospel, applied to our hearts every day, frees us to be brutally honest with ourselves and with God. The assurance of His total forgiveness of our sins through the blood of Christ means we don't have to play defensive games anymore. We don't have to rationalize and excuse our sins. We can say we told a lie instead of saying we exaggerated a bit. We can admit an unforgiving spirit instead of continuing to blame our parents for our emotional distress. We can call sin exactly what it is, regardless of how ugly and shameful it may be, because we know that Jesus bore that sin in His body on the cross. With the assurance of total forgiveness through Christ, we have no reason to hide from our sins anymore.

"But," you may be saying, "is it good to keep preaching the gospel to Christians who sin over and over again, who never seem to get their spiritual act together? Won't this cause them to quit trying? Won't they say, 'What's the use of struggling with my sin and lack of discipline? I'm forgiven anyway'? Don't we need a little bit of performance mentality to keep a sharp edge on our Christian commitment? And besides, what about all those indifferent Christians who never struggle with their sin and lack of commitment to Christ? Won't this emphasis on the gospel just harden them in their abuse of God's grace, their attitude that 'It doesn't matter how I live because God loves me unconditionally'?"

Let's consider the latter group of people first. It is true that God's grace can be abused. Paul anticipated that possibility (Romans 6:1, Galatians 5:13), and Jude indicated it was already happening in the first-century church (Jude 4). But we cannot allow some people's abuse of the truth to deprive us of its value to us, especially when that truth is so necessary to our Christian lives.

As to the first group—those who may be struggling with their sin and failure—the last thing they need is to have more guilt laid upon them. Few things cut the nerve of desire and earnest effort to change like a sense of guilt. On the contrary, freedom from guilt through the realization of forgiveness in Christ usually strengthens a person's desire to lead a more disciplined and holy life. And it is this deepened desire that will lead to earnest prayer for the Spirit's aid and a more diligent effort to pursue discipline and holiness.

Years ago I heard a godly minister say, "Discipline without desire is drudgery." What is it, then, that sparks the desire in our hearts to lead a disciplined, godly life? It is the joy of knowing that our sins are forgiven, that no matter how much we've stumbled and fallen today, God does not count our sins against us (Romans 4:8).

MOTIVATED BY LOVE

The Apostle Paul wrote that Christ died that we should no longer live for ourselves but for Him (2 Corinthians 5:15). To live no longer for ourselves but for Him is the essence of discipleship. That phrase sums up all we could include under the headings of disciplines, holiness, and service. But what is it that will motivate us to live not for ourselves but for Him? Paul said it is the love of Christ: "For Christ's love compels us" (2 Corinthians 5:14).

The idea behind the word *compel* is to press in upon so as to *impel*, that is, to urge or drive forward by the exertion of a strong moral pressure. Kenneth Wuest, in his expanded translation of the New Testament, beautifully captured the flavor of the word *compel*, as Paul used it here, when he translated, "For the love which Christ has [for me] presses on me from all sides, holding me to one end and prohibiting me from considering any other, wrapping itself around me in tenderness, giving me an impelling motive."[4]

Notice though, what compelled or motivated Paul in such a strong manner. It was not a continual challenge to be more disciplined, or more committed, or more holy. Rather it was his constant heartfelt awareness of Christ's love for him. It was not the thought that "I ought to do this or that" or a feeling of guilt for not doing something that motivated Paul. Rather it was his overwhelming sense of Christ's love for him that spurred him on.

We believers do need to be challenged to a life of committed discipleship, but that challenge needs to be based on the gospel, not on duty or guilt. Duty or guilt may motivate us for awhile, but only a sense of Christ's love for us will motivate us for a lifetime.

If the love of Christ for us is to be the motivating force for a life of discipleship, how then can we come to the place where we are acutely conscious of His love? The answer is, through the gospel. It is, of course, the Holy Spirit who pours out His love into our hearts (Romans 5:5), but He does this through the message of the gospel. The good news of the gospel is that Jesus paid for all our sins on the cross and that we are thereby forgiven. As we continually reflect upon that gospel, the Holy Spirit floods our hearts with a sense of God's love to us in Christ. And that sense of His love motivates us in a compelling way to live for Him.

Over the years many devoted Christians have been drawn to Paul's heartfelt desire expressed in Philippians 3:10, "that I may know him" (KJV). Our hearts have resonated with Paul's as we have said, "That's my desire, too, just to know Christ in a more personal and intimate way." What then is the immediate context of Paul's words? What is it that caused him to have such an intense yearning?

The context is Paul's testimony of how he renounced his own self-righteousness in order to gain the righteousness that comes from God through faith in Jesus Christ (Philippians 3:1-9). It is in the context of recounting the gospel as it applies to him personally that Paul feels this surge of desire to know Christ more intimately welling up within him.

A sense of obligation and duty never stimulates such a desire within us. Only love does that. If we are going to persevere as committed disciples of Jesus Christ over the course of our lives, we must always keep the gospel of God's forgiveness through Christ before us. We should, to use the words of my friend Jack Miller, preach the gospel to ourselves every day.

Preaching the gospel to ourselves every day addresses both the self-righteous Pharisee and the guilt-laden sinner that dwell in our hearts. Since the gospel is only for sinners, preaching it to ourselves every day reminds us that we are indeed sinners in need of God's grace. It causes us to say to God, in the words of an old hymn, "Nothing in my hands I bring, simply to thy cross I cling." It helps us to consciously renounce any confidence in our own goodness as a means of meriting God's blessing on our lives.

Perhaps more importantly, though, preaching the gospel to ourselves every day gives us hope, joy, and courage. The good news that our sins are forgiven because of Christ's death fills our hearts with joy, gives us courage to face the day, and offers us hope that God's favor will rest upon us, not because we are good, but because we are in Christ.

Several months prior to writing this chapter, I was given a copy of a letter written by Mutua Mahiaini, the leader of The Navigators ministry in Kenya, Africa, to The Navigators constituency in Kenya. In his letter, Mutua addresses rather eloquently this issue of performance versus God's grace, so I wrote him asking for permission to quote his letter. He kindly consented, so I quote most of it here for you.

> We know, of course, how central the forgiveness of our sins is to salvation. We preach it, we believe in it. We see that first repentance and surrender to Christ as a glorious moment. We also accept that having come to the Lord, we must continue to purify our lives. "If we confess our sins, He is faithful and just and will forgive us our sins and purify us from all unrighteousness." 1 John 1:9. But in talking with many believers, I get the impression that most of us consider the on-going repentance of the saved as a not-so-glorious experience. A sort of sad necessity.
>
> Sin grieves God. We must not down-play the seriousness of it in the life of a believer. But we must come to terms with the fact that God's Grace is GREATER THAN ALL OUR SINS. Repentance is one of the Christian's highest privileges. A repentant Christian focuses on God's mercy and God's grace. Any

moment in our lives when we bask in God's mercy and grace is our highest moment. Higher than when we feel snug in our decent performance and cannot think of anything we need to confess.

Whenever we fail—and fail we will, the Spirit of God will work on us and bring us to the foot of the cross where Jesus carried our failures. That is potentially a glorious moment. For we could at that moment accept God's abundant Mercy and Grace and go forth with nothing to boast of except Christ Himself, or else we struggle with our shame, focusing on that as well as our track record. We fail because we have shifted our attention from Grace and Mercy. One who draws on God's Mercy and Grace is quick to repent, but also slow to sin.[5]

Note Mutua's statement that any moment when we bask in God's mercy and grace is our highest moment, higher than when we feel snug in our decent performance and cannot think of anything we need to confess. Does that not remind you of Paul's words, "May I never boast except in the cross of our Lord Jesus Christ" (Galatians 6:14)?

Are you and I willing to live like Mutua and the Apostle Paul? Are we willing to rely on God's grace and mercy alone instead of our performance, to boast in nothing except the Cross? If so, then we can stop living in our good-day–bad-day scenarios and bask every day in the grace of God. And in the joy and confidence of that grace we can vigorously pursue holiness.

2

THE PHARISEE AND THE TAX COLLECTOR

"The Pharisee stood up and prayed about himself:
'God, I thank you that I am not like all other men—robbers,
evildoers, adulterers—or even like this tax collector.
I fast twice a week and give a tenth of all I get.'"
LUKE 18:11-12

ON HIS SEVENTIETH BIRTHDAY, pioneer missionary William Carey wrote to one of his sons these words:

I am this day seventy years old, a monument of Divine mercy and goodness, though on a review of my life I find much, very much, for which I ought to be humbled in the dust; my direct and positive sins are innumerable, my negligence in the Lord's work has been great, I have not promoted his cause, nor sought his glory and honour as I ought, notwithstanding all this, I am spared till now, and am still retained in his Work, and I trust I am received into the divine favour through him.[1]

Carey, who went to India in 1793, is often called the father of modern missions. His vast labors for Christ included translation of all or parts of the Bible into more than forty languages and dialects. He was the originator of the well-known missionary slogan "Expect great things from God; attempt great things for God."

How then could a man of such remarkable faith in God, who had accomplished so much for God, lament toward the end of his life his own sinfulness and shortcomings? Why would Carey not rather reflect with gratitude and praise on what God had done through him? Was Carey's attitude due to an unhealthy, low self-esteem, or did it reflect a healthy realism that is characteristic of a godly, mature Christian? Should Carey's attitude be an example for us to follow, or should we write it off as an unfortunate bit of introspection that comes with old age?

These are not just theoretical questions, because Carey's attitude addresses two significant needs among committed believers: the need for a humble realization of our own sinfulness, and the need for a grateful acceptance of God's grace.[2] Christians tend toward one of two opposite attitudes. The first is a relentless sense of guilt due to unmet expectations in living the Christian life. People characterized by this mode of thinking frequently dwell on their besetting sins or on their failure to witness to their neighbors or to live up to numerous other challenges of the Christian life that are so often laid upon them.

CHRISTIAN PHARISAISM
The other attitude is one of varying degrees of self-satisfaction with one's Christian life. We can drift into this attitude because we are convinced we believe the right doctrines, we read the right Christian books, we practice the right disciplines of a committed Christian life, or we are actively involved in some aspect of Christian ministry and are not just "pew sitters" in the church.

Perhaps we have become self-righteous about our Christian lives because we look at society around us and see flagrant immorality, pervasive dishonesty, wholesale greed, and increasing violence. We see growing acceptance of abortion as a "right" and homosexuality as an acceptable alternate lifestyle. Because we are not guilty of these more gross forms of sin, we can begin to feel rather good about our Christian lives.

When we think in this manner we are in danger of becoming like the Pharisee in Jesus' well-known parable (Luke 18:9-14). Jesus said, "The Pharisee stood up and prayed about himself: 'God, I thank you that I am not like other men—robbers, evildoers, adulterers—or even like this tax collector. I fast twice a week and give a tenth of all I get'" (verses 11-12).

The Pharisee was orthodox in his beliefs and very committed in his religious practices. He would have met our threefold description of discipleship. He fasted twice a week (spiritual disciplines); he was not a robber, evildoer, or adulterer (obedience); and he gave a tenth of all his income (service). To use our good-day–bad-day terminology, he was living in a continuous good-day scenario, or so he thought. But he had one fatal flaw. He was self-righteous and, through Jesus' parable, has become the classic example of religious pride and self-satisfaction.

Unlike the Pharisee, the tax collector was painfully aware of his sinfulness. He didn't just ask for forgiveness of certain sins; he pleaded for mercy as a sinner. In the original language, the text reads, "God be merciful to me *the* sinner." Not only did he not compare himself favorably with others as the Pharisee did; he didn't compare himself at all. He was not concerned with how he measured up with respect to other people. He was concerned with how he measured up before a holy and righteous God. He knew he stood alone before God with his sin, so he pleaded for mercy.

Jesus said the tax collector went home justified, or declared righteous, before God. He freely and rather desperately acknowledged that he had no righteousness of his own, so he received his as a gift from God.

We usually approach this story with the sense of approval that comes from reading about other people instead of ourselves. We agree that the Pharisee was dripping with religious pride, but then we think the parable doesn't apply to us because we have trusted in Christ and are already justified. We shouldn't, however, relegate this parable just to the self-righteous and obvious "sinners" among unbelievers. The parable also speaks to us who are believers.

Jesus told the parable to those who were confident of their own righteousness, that is, to those who felt good about their own performance. As long as we compare ourselves with society around us and with other believers who are not as committed as we are, we also are apt to become confident of our own righteousness—not a righteousness unto salvation, but at least a righteousness that will make God pleased with our performance. The sin of the Pharisee, then, can become the sin of the most orthodox and committed Christian.

A large part of our problem as evangelical believers is that we have defined sin in its more obvious forms—forms of which we are not guilty. We think of sin in terms of sexual immorality, drunkenness, lying, cheating, stealing, and murder. And in more recent years we've tended to focus on the societal sins of abortion and homosexuality. We see the ever-increasing pervasiveness of these more flagrant sins, and we see ourselves looking good by comparison.

Certainly these more gross sins of society are deep cause for concern, and I am grateful for the prophetic voices God has raised up to expose these moral cancers in our society. But we must not become so preoccupied with the sins of modern-day culture that we ignore the needs in our own lives.

REFINED SINS
Most often our sin problem is in the area I call "refined" sins. These are the sins of nice people, sins that we can regularly commit and still retain our positions as elders, deacons, Sunday school teachers, Bible study leaders, and yes, even full-time Christian workers.

What are some of these "refined" sins? As I looked at my own life, one of the first that came to mind was the tendency to judge others and to speak critically of them to other people. That this sin came to mind so quickly surprised me, because I don't think of myself as a critical or judgmental person. Perhaps that is part of the problem. This seems to be such an acceptable vice among believers that we don't even recognize it unless it is flagrant—and always in someone else.

We need to take seriously Jesus' warning about a critical spirit in Matthew 7:3: "Why do you look at the speck of sawdust in your brother's eye and pay no attention to the plank in your own eye?" We need to learn to back off from judging others and leave that to God, as the Apostle Paul instructed us when he said, "Who are you to judge someone else's servant? To his own master he stands or falls. And he will stand, for the Lord is able to make him stand" (Romans 14:4). A judgmental spirit is too often a vice of committed Christians. We need to recognize it as the sin it really is.

A judgmental spirit usually reflects itself in speech that is critical of others. It was with dismay that I realized some months ago that I needed to begin praying David's prayer:

> Set a guard over my mouth, O LORD;
> keep watch over the door of my lips. (Psalm 141:3)

As the Holy Spirit began working on me in this area, I was surprised to realize how often I was saying something critical of another brother or sister in Christ.

Closely akin to judgmental speech is gossip, that endless recounting and passing on of the sins and misfortunes of others. We seem to get a perverse delight out of being the bearer of bad news about other people. Solomon warned us about gossip when he said,

> He who covers over an offense promotes love,
> but whoever repeats the matter separates close
> friends. (Proverbs 17:9)

And again,

> A gossip betrays a confidence;
>   so avoid a man who talks too much.
>   (Proverbs 20:19)

Do we take Solomon seriously, or more accurately, do we take the Holy Spirit seriously—for, after all, Solomon wrote under His inspiration and guidance?

The Apostle Paul wrote, "Do not let any unwholesome talk come out of your mouths, but only what is helpful for building others up according to their needs, that it may benefit those who listen" (Ephesians 4:29). The word *unwholesome* covers any type of speech that tends to tear down another person, either spoken to or about that person. And Paul's prohibition against this type of negative speech is absolute: "Do not let *any* unwholesome talk come out of your mouths, but *only* what is helpful for building others up" (emphasis added).

How would we respond if someone said, "Well, I'm really not a thief, but I do steal occasionally," or "I'm not an adulterer, but I sometimes have an affair"? We would find such an attitude ridiculous and unacceptable for a believer. We know God's prohibitions against stealing and adultery are absolute. But all too often we allow ourselves to think this way about our speech. We engage in gossip and criticism, though we wouldn't want to be known as a gossip or a critical person.

The Scriptures do not allow for *any* gossip or criticism, or any other form of unwholesome speech, even if what we say is true. We are simply not to say anything about someone else that we wouldn't want to eventually reach that person's ear.

Even criticism addressed *to* someone should be given only with the goal of benefiting that person. It should never be given out of a spirit of impatience or irritability, or with a desire to belittle the individual. Only honest criticism given from a heart of love in a spirit of humility can qualify as that which builds up the other person.

Which of us, then, does not offend frequently with our tongue? The real problem, however, is not our tongues but our hearts. Jesus said, "For out of the overflow of the heart the mouth speaks" (Matthew 12:34). So it would not be sufficient to win control over our tongues, even if we could. We must recognize the sin in our hearts.

What are some other "refined" sins that we can commit and still be respectable among our Christian friends? Some of the more common ones are in the area of interpersonal relationships. These would include resentment, bitterness, an unforgiving spirit, impatience, and irritability. It is very instructive that it is in the context of interpersonal relationships that Paul wrote his warning, "And do not grieve the Holy Spirit of God" (Ephesians 4:30). Now, all sin grieves God, and Paul could have inserted that warning in the context of sexual immorality (Ephesians 5:3-5) or lying and stealing (Ephesians 4:25,28). But he places it in the context of sins we commit with hardly any sense of shame or guilt. The message should be clear. God is grieved over our "refined" sins just as He is grieved over sexual immorality or dishonesty. I am not suggesting that being irritable at one's spouse is as serious as something like adultery. I am saying that being irritable at one's spouse is sin, and that *all* sin grieves God and should grieve us.

One of our problems with these so-called refined sins is that we have become too comfortable with the whole concept of sin. Because we do sin so frequently we learn to coexist with it as long as it doesn't get too out of control or scandalous. We forget, or perhaps have never learned, how seriously God regards all sin.

THE SERIOUSNESS OF SIN

Three passages of Scripture that have helped me see the seriousness of sin are Leviticus 16:21, 2 Samuel 12:9-12, and 1 Kings 13:21, as these are translated in the *New International*

Version. In Leviticus 16:21, God uses the word *rebellion* to describe the sins of the Israelites. The Hebrew word, which is usually translated as "transgression," means rebellion against authority. So God considers our sin, be it refined or scandalous, as rebellion against His sovereign rule over His creatures.

The 2 Samuel 12:9-10 passage occurs in the prophet Nathan's rebuke of David for committing adultery with Bathsheba and then having her husband killed in an attempt to cover up his sin. There God says through Nathan that David had despised His Word (verse 9), and even God Himself (verse 10). The word *despise* means to disdain or treat with contempt. So, when we sin we are in effect treating God and His Word with disdain or contempt; we are despising Him.

We cannot evade the force of the word *despise*, thinking it fits the scandalous nature of David's crimes but doesn't apply to us. The same God who said, "You shall not murder" or "You shall not commit adultery" also said, "You shall not covet" (Exodus 20:13-14,17). It is not the seriousness of the sin as we view it, but the infinite majesty and sovereignty of the God who gave the commands, that makes our sin a despising of God and His Word. Even as I write these words I bow my head in shame to realize how lightly I have treated some sins that God regards as rebellion and a despising of Him.

The third word, which occurs in 1 Kings 13:21, is *defy*: "You have defied the word of the LORD." The word *disobeyed*, used in this instance in most Bible translations, doesn't capture the intense force of this word, probably because we are so used to the concept of disobedience. But we all recognize that the word *defy* escalates the seriousness of disobedience. It is a direct challenge to authority.

That God would use such a word in this instance is all the more striking because the prophet who defied God didn't commit a scandalous sin. He simply did what God had specifically told him not to do—to eat or drink in the land of Samaria or return by the way he came. Yet God regarded his sin not as mere disobedience on the level we associate with that word but as defiance. Again, the seriousness of sin is not simply measured by its consequences, but by the authority of the One who gives the command.

So these three words—*rebellion, despise,* and *defy*—are all synonyms for sin that can help us begin to grasp the seriousness of all sin, even our so-called refined sins. And we are not through yet.

As we continue to probe the sinfulness of our hearts, we come to self-centeredness; selfish ambition; the love of position, power, or praise; an independent spirit; and the tendency to manipulate events or other people for our own ends. Then there is indifference to the eternal or temporal welfare of those around us, and finally the cancerous sin of materialism.

I know that we get a lot of guilt laid on us in the United States about materialism, and I have no desire to lay guilt on someone just because he or she lives in a better house and eats better food than people in the less developed countries. But I recently heard a statistic that both alarmed and saddened me: Only 4 percent of evangelicals in the United States give a tithe (10 percent) of their income to God's work.

Even though some Christians question the applicability of the tithe concept in the New Testament era, this is still a shameful statistic. It means the overwhelming majority of professing Christians in the most affluent nation in history are spending most of their income on themselves.

On the other hand, those of us who do give 10 percent or more of our income to God's work can become proud and self-righteous about it as we look around and see others who are not as generous. In that case, all we are doing is exchanging one sin for another—the sin of materialism and selfishness for the sin of self-righteous pride.

We could mention a score of other sins—those of the mind and heart that no one else knows about except God. But we have not even mentioned our failures to exhibit the positive traits of Christian character, such as love, gentleness, kindness, patience, and humility. We are not only to put off the traits of the old self, we are also to put on the traits of the new self (see Ephesians 4:22-24).

POSITIVE CHARACTER TRAITS

Several months before writing this chapter, I went through most of the New Testament compiling a list of positive character traits taught and enjoined upon us by Jesus and the apostles, either by direct teaching or by example. I found twenty-seven such traits.[3] I was not surprised by the frequent references to love and the conclusion that love is undoubtedly the primary Christian character trait. After all, Jesus did say that love to God and to our neighbor are the first and second commandments (Matthew 22:37-39).

It is easy to consent to the primacy of love and yet so difficult to practice it. Some years ago, in an effort to help me put "shoe leather" to the concept of love, I stated a couple of verses from the great love chapter, 1 Corinthians 13, as action statements. As you read over these action statements from verses 4 and 5, ask yourself how you are doing in your day-to-day practice of love. Is there any room for self-righteousness in the light of this practical standard of love?

❖ I am patient with you because I love you and want to forgive you.

❖ I am kind to you because I love you and want to help you.

❖ I do not envy your possessions or your gifts because I love you and want you to have the best.

❖ I do not boast about my attainments because I love you and want to hear about yours.

❖ I am not proud because I love you and want to esteem you before myself.

❖ I am not rude because I love you and care about your feelings.

❖ I am not self-seeking because I love you and want

to meet your needs.

✤ I am not easily angered by you because I love you and want to overlook your offenses.

✤ I do not keep a record of your wrongs because I love you, and "love covers a multitude of sins."[4]

While not surprised by the primacy of love in New Testament teaching, I was surprised by the almost forty references to humility, either in the use of the word itself or in concept, and the obvious importance both Jesus and the apostles put on that virtue. Yet how little attention do most of us give to growing in humility. The opposite trait of humility, of course, is pride, and there is no pride like that of self-righteousness, feeling good about our own religious performance and looking down on others'.

Jesus not only gave us the story of the Pharisee and the tax collector, but also the story of the prodigal son (see Luke 15:11-32). The emphasis of that story is, of course, on the love, compassion, and grace of the son's father. Jesus could have stopped, however, at the point in the story of the father's forgiveness and glad celebration over the return of his son. As far as the father's compassion was concerned, Jesus' point would have been made. But He didn't stop there. He proceeded to tell us about the jealousy and resentment of the self-righteous older brother.

Jesus' criticism of the older brother is implied rather than stated. But it is obvious that He puts the older brother in the same category as the self-righteous Pharisee. Yet the older brother would have qualified as an elder or deacon in any of our churches today and would have been highly regarded. We need to learn the lesson Jesus was teaching and to see the hideousness of the sin of self-righteousness.

The problem with self-righteousness is that it seems almost impossible to recognize in ourselves. We will own up to almost any other sin, but not the sin of self-righteousness. When we have this attitude, though, we deprive ourselves of the joy of living in the grace of God. Because,

✳ you see, grace is only for sinners.

After love and humility, there are at least twenty-five more Christian virtues to put on, among which there is surely a lot of room for all of us to grow. Yet to the extent that we miss the mark in those positive Christian character traits, we are sinners in need of God's grace.

SAINTS OR SINNERS?

I am sometimes asked, "As Christians, should we view ourselves as saints or sinners?" My answer is, both. We are simultaneously saints and sinners. The Apostle Paul often referred to believers as saints (Ephesians 1:1, Philippians 1:1, etc.), and we really are. We are saints not only in our standing before God but in our essential persons as well.

We really are new creations in Christ. A real, fundamental change has occurred in the depths of our beings. The Holy Spirit has come to dwell within us, and we have been freed from the dominion of sin. But despite this we still sin every day, many times a day. And in that sense we are sinners.

We should always view ourselves both in terms of what we are in Christ, that is, saints, and what we are in ourselves, namely, sinners. To help us understand this twofold view of ourselves, consider Jesus as an analogy. In His own person He was sinless, but as our representative He assumed our guilt. However, He never had any of the personal feelings associated with guilt. He was fully conscious of His own sinlessness even when bearing our sins and the curse of our sins in our place. In like manner, while we should always rejoice in the righteousness we have in Christ, we should never cease to feel deeply our own sinfulness and consequent unworthiness.

In other words, just as Christ could maintain a separate sense of His personal sinlessness and His official bearing of our sin, so we must distinguish between the righteousness we have in Him and the sinfulness we see in ourselves.

If we refuse to identify ourselves as sinners as well as saints, we risk the danger of deceiving ourselves about our sin and becoming like the self-righteous Pharisee. Our hearts are deceitful (Jeremiah 17:9), and we all have moral "blind spots." We have a difficult enough time seeing our sin without someone insisting that we no longer consider ourselves as "sinners."

INTROSPECTION OR HONEST CANDOR?

Let's return to the letter William Carey wrote to his son. Was Carey objective and realistic when he wrote of his positive sins, which were innumerable, or was he just overly introspective? If he was not unduly introspective, was he an example of a mature Christian, or was he actually more sinful than the typical evangelical of today? The answers to these questions should be obvious to us by now. But are we willing to humbly admit our own sinfulness, as Carey did? I'm not referring to the confession of specific sins during the course of a day but to an acknowledgment of our own tenacious sinfulness, the state of our hearts.

While working on this chapter I came across the following paragraph written in our own time, almost two hundred years after William Carey wrote his letter to his son.

> I write these words at the age of fifty-five. During the past ten or twelve years, I have often—and with greater seriousness than ever before—reflected upon the course of my life. Certain patterns of thought and attitude and conduct have come to light, some of them quite disturbing. I look back upon repeated failures in my efforts to subdue inner conflicts and fears, to combat immaturity and self-centeredness, to build genuine and enriching relationships with other people, to conquer besetting sins, and to grow in holiness and communion with God. I now see that every period of my life has been marked by . . . struggle. But the persistence of the failures, together with a growing understanding of the past, has made the struggles of recent years exceptionally intense and painful.[5]

These words were not written by a so-called defeated Christian but by a seminary professor respected by both his colleagues and students for his humble and devoted walk with God. What a rare expression of humility and candor. Most of us wouldn't even speak those words about ourselves in public, let alone commit them to print. Yet those are the words of a man who knows what it is to live by the grace of God instead of his own performance.

Consider the example of the Apostle Paul. He not only referred to himself as the least of the apostles, not even deserving to be called an apostle, but he considered himself less than the least of all God's people (1 Corinthians 15:9, Ephesians 3:8). And toward the end of his life he referred to himself as the worst of sinners and as a monument to the unlimited patience of Jesus Christ (1 Timothy 1:15-16). If ever there was a person who excelled in the disciplines of the Christian life, in obedience, and in sacrificial service, surely it was Paul. Yet he viewed himself in a manner similar to William Carey and the seminary professor.

What's the point of all this? Well, whom do we identify with, the Pharisee or the tax collector, the prodigal son or the older brother? Obviously no one wants to identify with the Pharisee or the older brother. But are we willing to identify with the tax collector and the prodigal son, as sinners deeply in need of the grace and mercy of God? Are we willing to say, "God be merciful to me *the* sinner" or "I am no longer worthy to be called your son"? Are we willing to acknowledge that even our righteous acts are no more than filthy rags in the sight of God (Isaiah 64:6)?

John Owen, known as the prince of Puritan theologians, wrote these words way back in 1657:

> Believers obey Christ as the one by whom our obedience is accepted by God. Believers know all their duties are weak, imperfect and unable to abide in God's presence. Therefore they look to Christ as the one who bears the iniquity of their holy things, who

adds incense to their prayers, gathers out all the weeds from their duties and makes them acceptable to God.[6]

Note that Owen speaks of Christ bearing the iniquity of our holy things—that is, the sinfulness of even our good works. As another Puritan preacher was reputed to have said, "Even our tears of repentance need to be washed in the blood of the Lamb." So our best works can never earn us one bit of favor with God. Let us then turn our attention from our own performance, whether it seems good or bad to us, and look to the gospel of Jesus Christ, which is God's provision for our sin, not only on the day we trusted Christ for our salvation but every day of our Christian lives.

3

PREACH THE GOSPEL TO YOURSELF

*Therefore, there is now no condemnation
for those who are in Christ Jesus.*

ROMANS 8:1

SOMETIME DURING 1993, a survey was taken on the floor of a large Christian convention attended by several thousand people. One of the survey questions was, "What is the gospel?" Of the scores of people interviewed, only one gave what could be considered an adequate answer.[1]

During the same time period, I was in contact with two men in different parts of the country regarding conferences where I was to speak. As we discussed the messages I was to deliver, both men said to me, "The people here don't know what the gospel is." Yet both groups I was to address were in the mainstream of evangelicalism.

Does this mean these people are not Christians? No, I would not make such a judgment on the basis of someone's ability to clearly articulate the gospel. As an elder in our local church I have participated in a number of interviews of prospective members. Frequently I have observed that many people, though clearly believers, have only a very elementary knowledge of the gospel.

45

At the same time, however, these observations constitute a serious indictment of our evangelical discipling process. The gospel is not only the most important message in all of history; it is the only essential message in all of history. Yet we allow thousands of professing Christians to live their entire lives without clearly understanding it and experiencing the joy of living by it.

I believe part of the problem is our tendency to give an unbeliever just enough of the gospel to get him or her to pray a prayer to receive Christ. Then we immediately put the gospel on the shelf, so to speak, and go on to the duties of discipleship. As a result, Christians are not instructed in the gospel. And because they do not fully understand the riches and glory of the gospel, they cannot preach it to themselves, nor live by it in their daily lives.

In chapter 1, I stated that the typical evangelical paradigm is that the gospel is for unbelievers and the duties of discipleship are for believers. But the gospel is for believers also, and we must pursue holiness, or any other aspect of discipleship, in the atmosphere of the gospel. To do that, however, we must firmly grasp what the gospel is and what it means in practical terms to preach it to ourselves every day.

With that in mind, we will thoroughly review the gospel in this chapter, paying attention to its application to our daily lives as believers. So don't skip over this chapter because you consider yourself thoroughly grounded in the gospel. Rather, look at it this time from the viewpoint of its application to your daily life as a believer.

THE GOSPEL

The single passage in all of the Bible that most clearly and completely explains the gospel is Romans 3:19-26. A minister friend of mine calls this passage "The Heart of the Gospel." So if we are going to preach the gospel to ourselves every day and learn to live by it, we need to understand Romans 3:19-26. To help us examine that passage, I will quote it here in its entirety.

Now we know that whatever the law says, it says to those who are under the law, so that every mouth may be silenced and the whole world held accountable to God. Therefore no one will be declared righteous in his sight by observing the law; rather, through the law we become conscious of sin. But now a righteousness from God, apart from law, has been made known, to which the Law and the Prophets testify. This righteousness from God comes through faith in Jesus Christ to all who believe. There is no difference, for all have sinned and fall short of the glory of God, and are justified freely by his grace through the redemption that came by Christ Jesus. God presented him as a sacrifice of atonement, through faith in his blood. He did this to demonstrate his justice, because in his forbearance he had left the sins committed beforehand unpunished— he did it to demonstrate his justice at the present time, so as to be just and the one who justifies those who have faith in Jesus.

As we look over this statement of the gospel, we can see seven truths that we need to clearly understand:

No One Is Declared Righteous Before God by Observing the Law (Verses 19-21)

The word *righteous* means exact and perfect conformity to the law of God. When I use the term *the law of God* here, I am not referring specifically to the law given to the nation of Israel through Moses. Rather, I am using the term in a more general sense to refer to the transcript of God's nature and the rule of obedience that He requires of all human beings. It includes all of the ethical commands scattered throughout the Bible.

The standard of obedience required by the law is absolute perfection, for James 2:10 tells us, "For whoever keeps the whole law and yet stumbles at just one point is guilty of breaking all of it." The Apostle Paul said essentially the same thing when he wrote, "All who rely on observing the law are under a curse, for it is written: 'Cursed is everyone who does not continue to do everything written in the Book of the Law'" (Galatians 3:10).

Only perfect obedience is acceptable to God. Years ago Ivory soap had a slogan, "Ninety-nine-and-forty-four-one-hundredths-percent pure." Apparently that is quite an accomplishment for soap, but that is not good enough for God. Only 100 percent is acceptable. Yet the average person walking around today, if he or she has thought about it at all, is confident God will accept him or her because he or she is generally a decent sort of person.

As Christians we know better. We readily acknowledge that we can never through our own obedience attain a righteousness that is sufficient for salvation. But then as believers we act as if we can live lives acceptable to God. Think of the good-day–bad-day scenarios I described in chapter 1. More than 80 percent of the people I've questioned in a group setting indicate they would be more confident of God's blessing when they've had a "good" day. None of them, however, would claim 100-percent obedience. Not one of them would want to stake his or her hope for eternal life on his or her performance on the very best day. Yet, in our everyday relationship with God, most of us are no different in our thinking than the unbelievers who think they will go to Heaven because they've been good enough. To live by grace, we must rid ourselves of such thinking.

There Is a Righteousness from God That Is Apart from Law (Verse 21)

Since we cannot attain a sufficient righteousness on our own, God has provided it for us. This righteousness from God is none other than the perfect righteousness of Jesus Christ, who through His sinless life and His death in obedience to the Father's will, perfectly fulfilled the law of God. That is, the righteousness that is a gift from God is a real righteousness, worked out in a real world, by a real person, the

Lord Jesus Christ. It is nothing less than perfect conformity to the law of God over a period of thirty-three years by the Son of God, who became a human being and lived a life of perfect obedience.

The righteousness of Jesus Christ is as much a historical reality as is the fact of sin, and in the book of Romans they are set in contrast to one another; that is, Adam's sin over against Christ's righteousness (see Romans 5:12-19). Nineteenth-century Scottish theologian George Smeaton wrote, "[The Apostle Paul] exhibits the two great counterparts of sin and righteousness as equal realities—the one as the world's ruin, the other as its restoration. The one is a completed fact as well as the other. They are the only two great events or facts in the world's history, and they confront each other."[2]

It is important to realize that our Lord Jesus Christ perfectly fulfilled the law of God, both in its requirements and its penalty. He did what Adam failed to do—render perfect obedience to the law of God. Then by His death He completely paid the penalty of a broken law. So, from the standpoint of obedience to the law and of paying the penalty for breaking the law, He perfectly fulfilled the law of God.

Therefore when God justifies us, or declares us righteous, He does not create some sort of legal fiction, calling something righteous that is not. Rather, He declares us righteous on the basis of the real, accomplished righteousness of Jesus Christ, which is imputed or credited to us through faith.

Another Scotsman, Robert Haldane (1764–1842), author of a masterful commentary on Romans, wrote these words about the righteousness of Christ: "To that righteousness is the eye of the believer ever to be directed; on that righteousness must he rest; on that righteousness must he live; on that righteousness must he die; in that righteousness must he appear before the judgment-seat; in that righteousness must he stand for ever in the presence of a righteous God."[3]

The righteousness of Jesus Christ is imputed or credited to us forever. From the day we trust in Christ as our Savior, on throughout eternity, we stand before God clothed in the righteousness of Jesus Christ. Isaiah the prophet spoke of this righteousness when he wrote,

> I delight greatly in the LORD;
>> my soul rejoices in my God.
> For he has clothed me with garments of salvation
>> and arrayed me in a robe of righteousness,
> as a bridegroom adorns his head like a priest,
>> and as a bride adorns herself with her jewels.
>> (Isaiah 61:10)

This standing in Christ's righteousness is never affected to any degree by our good-day or bad-day performance. Unless we learn to live daily by faith in (that is, by reliance on) His righteousness, however, our *perception* of our standing before God will vary depending on our good or bad performance.

This Righteousness from God Is Received Through Faith in Jesus Christ (Verse 22)

Faith is the hand by which the righteousness of Christ is received. Faith itself has no merit; in fact, by its nature it is self-emptying. It involves our complete renunciation of any confidence in our own righteousness and a relying entirely on the perfect righteousness and death of Jesus Christ.

This twofold aspect of faith—renunciation and reliance—is vividly demonstrated in the evangelism training offered by Evangelism Explosion. The person presenting the gospel to an unbeliever is instructed to denote the chair on which he or she is sitting as representing reliance on one's own goodness for salvation. An adjacent, empty chair is designated to represent reliance on Jesus Christ. The presenter of the gospel then moves from the chair representing one's goodness to the chair representing faith in Jesus Christ while pointing out that it is impossible to sit on both chairs at once. The point is then made that, in order to trust in Christ for one's salvation, one must completely abandon any trust in one's own goodness or merit. Faith in Christ and a reliance on ourselves, even to the smallest degree, are mutually exclusive.

The word *faith* is a noun and has no verbal form in English. Instead the word *believe* is used, as in Acts 16:31, "Believe in the Lord Jesus, and you will be saved." What does it mean to believe *in* Jesus, that is, what is it we are to believe? We are to believe that as the Son of God, clothed in our humanity, He lived a perfect life and then died on the cross for our sins. This message is called the gospel, that is, the good news about Jesus Christ.

Jesus Himself is always to be the object of our faith. We sometimes say we are saved by faith alone, meaning apart from any works. That expression, however, can be somewhat misleading, as though faith itself has some virtue that God respects. It is more accurate to say we are saved by God's grace through faith. Faith, again, is merely the hand that receives the gift of God, and God through His Spirit even opens our hand to receive the gift.

This doctrine of trusting in Jesus Christ alone for one's salvation is a basic truth of the gospel. Without acceptance of it there is no salvation. All believers by definition accept that fact. But it is important to realize that we were not only saved by faith at a particular point in time, but we are to live by faith in Christ every day of our lives. This means that, as shown in the Evangelism Explosion illustration with the two chairs, I must continue to renounce any confidence in my own goodness and place my confidence solely in Christ every day of my life, not only for my eternal salvation, but for my daily acceptance before a holy God.

The Apostle Paul wrote, "The life I live in the body, I live by faith in the Son of God, who loved me and gave himself for me" (Galatians 2:20). The context of Galatians 2:20 is justification—being declared righteous on the basis of the righteousness of Christ. So when Paul wrote that he lived by faith in the Son of God, he was not in that passage referring to a dependence on Christ for spiritual strength (as is the case in Philippians 4:13), but to a dependence on Him for his righteous standing before God on a day-to-day basis.

This Righteousness Is Available to Everyone on the Same Basis, Since All Have Sinned and Fall Short of the Glory of God (Verses 22-23)

God's plan of salvation treats all people equally, since all are sinners. This is not to say that God notices no distinction in the seriousness and aggravation of different sins. But as we saw in the previous chapter, any sin, however small and insignificant it may seem to us, is a violation of God's holy law and subjects us to the penalty of death.

One person may be a relatively decent sinner and another may be a flagrant sinner, but both are sinners, and God's law admits of no degree of failure. If sixty is the passing grade on a college exam, it does not matter if you scored forty and I scored only twenty. We both failed to get a passing grade. There is no point in your boasting that your failing grade is superior to mine. The only thing that matters is that we both failed the exam.

The first purpose of God's method of salvation through Christ's death is to deliver us from guilt, and though all people are not equally guilty, all *are* guilty. So, as Paul said, "There is no difference." Or, as a more contemporary expression says it, "The ground is level at the foot of the cross."

This eliminates any room for comparison of ourselves with others who may appear more sinful—or at least less holy—than we are. So if we are to live by the gospel every day, all tendency to compare ourselves with other believers, not to mention unbelievers, must be put away. Rather we must measure ourselves against God's perfect standard and daily confess that we have sinned and fallen short of the glory of God.

All Who Put Their Faith in Jesus Christ Are Justified Freely by God's Grace (Verse 24)

To be justified is to be absolved from any charge of guilt and to be declared absolutely righteous. We are not only discharged from all liability to God's wrath because of our guilt; we are personally accepted by God because of Christ. Justification is like the two sides of a coin. On the one side we are declared "not guilty" before God, and on the other we are positively declared to be righteous through Christ. That is, we are counted in God's sight as having perfectly obeyed the law of God.

We must keep in mind that our justification by God is based solely on the meritorious work of Christ and our union with Him.[4] That is, God sees us legally as so connected with Christ that what He did, we did. When He lived a life of perfect obedience, it is as if we had lived a life of perfect obedience. When He died on the cross to satisfy the just demands of God's law, it is just as if we had died on that cross. Christ stood in our place as our representative, both in His sinless life and His sin-bearing death. This is what Paul referred to when he said, "I have been crucified with Christ" (Galatians 2:20).

To live by the gospel, then, means that we firmly grasp the fact that Christ's life and death are ours by virtue of our union with Him. What He did, we did. This is the only sense in which we can understand Paul's bold statements in Romans 8: "Therefore, there is now no condemnation for those who are in Christ Jesus" (verse 1); "If God is for us, who can be against us?" (verse 31); and "Who will bring any charge against those whom God has chosen? It is God who justifies" (verse 33).

These statements by Paul are objective truths; that is, they are true whether we grasp them or not. So often, however, we find it difficult to believe them. Because of our frequent failures before God, we do feel under condemnation, we do not feel God is for us but rather must surely be against us, we do think He is bringing charges against us. At such times we must preach the gospel to ourselves. We must review what God has declared to be true about our justification in Christ.

Justification is a completed work as far as God is concerned. The penalty has been paid and His justice has been satisfied. But it must be received through faith and must be continually renewed in our souls and applied to our consciences every day through faith. There are two "courts" we must deal with: the court of God in Heaven and the court of conscience in our souls. When we trust in Christ for salvation, God's court is forever satisfied. Never again will a charge of guilt be brought against us in Heaven. Our consciences, however, are continually pronouncing us guilty. That is the function of conscience. Therefore, we must by faith bring the verdict of conscience into line with the verdict of Heaven. We do this by agreeing with our conscience about our guilt, but then reminding it that our guilt has already been borne by Christ.

This justification is said to be given to us freely by His grace. The word *freely* signifies without payment of any kind. Justification cannot be purchased by the payment of good works. There is no exchange of value between the sinner and God. It is an absolutely gratuitous act on His part. This freeness of justification was foretold by the prophet Isaiah:

> "Come, all you who are thirsty,
>   come to the waters;
> and you who have no money,
>   come, buy and eat!
> Come, buy wine and milk
>   without money and without cost." (Isaiah 55:1)

Grace, as we have already observed, is the undeserved favor of God shown to those who deserve His wrath. Grace presupposes guilt on our part. By definition, it is sovereign grace; that is, God is under no obligation to grant to any of us such undeserved favor. (In fact, God did not grant such favor to the angels that sinned [2 Peter 2:4].) The decision to grant such favor to us originated solely within His own goodness.

This Justification Is "Through the Redemption That Came by Christ Jesus" (Verse 24)

Charles Hodge, the famous professor of theology at Princeton Theological Seminary in the nineteenth century, said that redemption, as used in verse 24, means "deliverance effected by the payment of a ransom. . . . That from which we are redeemed is the wrath of God; the price of our redemption is the blood of Christ."[5] A few paragraphs earlier we saw that justification is a gratuitous act of God as far as we are concerned. But though it was totally free to us, it was in fact "purchased" by Christ with His blood. Christ paid the ransom that redeemed us from God's just and holy wrath.

At this point it will be helpful to distinguish between justification and a mere pardon. A pardon is excusing an offense without exacting a penalty. It may be granted gratuitously by a president or governor for no reason at all, and sometimes has been done at the expense of justice. For example, there was a great outcry when the late President Nixon was pardoned because many felt, rightly or wrongly, that justice had been violated by the granting of his pardon.

In God's plan of justification, however, justice is not violated by a gratuitous pardon of the convicted sinner. Rather, justice has been satisfied; the penalty has been fully paid by the Lord Jesus Christ. In a sense, to justify is to declare that the claims of justice have been fully met.

We need to dwell more on the work of Christ as it satisfied the demands of God's law. I once was given a book titled *The Satisfaction of Christ*. I opened it expecting it to be about finding satisfaction in my daily relationship with Christ. Instead, I discovered it to be about the death of Christ and how His death completely satisfied the justice of God. I had been a Christian for more than twelve years and had never before heard the expression "the satisfaction of Christ," let alone understood its significance.

The satisfaction of Christ is more than a mere theological expression. It is a concept we need to become acquainted with in our daily lives. When our consciences are smiting us because of our sin, it is important to reflect upon the fact that, though our sins are real and inexcusable, nevertheless God's justice has already been satisfied through the "satisfaction of Christ," that the penalty has been fully paid by Him.

"God Presented [Jesus] as a Sacrifice of Atonement Through Faith in His Blood" (Verse 25)

The *New International Version* footnote helps us understand the meaning of "sacrifice of atonement" with an alternate reading of "as the one who would turn aside his [God's] wrath, taking away sin." The atonement, then, assumes the wrath of God against sin, and our consequent liability to His holy and just wrath. Paul affirmed this quite clearly in Romans 1:18 when he said, "The wrath of God is being revealed from heaven against all the godlessness and wickedness of men," and then in Ephesians 2:3 where he said, "We were by nature objects of wrath." By the wrath of God, we should not understand uncontrolled passion and hatred. Rather, as the late British pastor, D. Martyn Lloyd-Jones, wrote, the wrath of God means "His settled opposition to all that is evil, arising out of His very nature. . . . His nature is such that He abhors evil, He hates evil. His holiness of necessity leads to that."[6]

Some Bible translations use the word *propitiation* where the New International Version says, "sacrifice of atonement." Though *propitiation* is seldom a part of our evangelical vocabulary today, it is a word with which all Christians ought to become familiar. Propitiation in the context of salvation means that which appeases the wrath of God against sin. So the Lord Jesus Christ by His sacrifice on the cross appeased and turned aside God's just and holy wrath, the wrath we should have borne.

We should notice two important points about this propitiatory act of Christ. First, God presented Him, or set Him forth as an atoning sacrifice. It is God the Father who initiated the whole plan of salvation. It is God the Father who provided the sacrifice of His Son to satisfy His justice and appease His own wrath. When we are acutely conscious of our sin and think that God's wrath must somehow be hanging over us, we need to remember that God the Father Himself is the One who devised a way whereby His wrath against sin might be fully executed apart from our experiencing the force of that wrath.

The second point is that this propitiation is appropriated by us as sinners through faith in His blood. The blood of Christ, referring to His death, is to be the object of our faith by which we appropriate His propitiation. "The blood of Christ," in connection with our salvation, is a favorite expression of New Testament writers, occurring about thirty times. It is the blood of Christ that cleanses our consciences from the defilement of sin (Hebrews 9:14); it is the blood of Christ that purifies us from all sin (1 John 1:7); it is by the blood of Christ that we have confidence to enter into the Most Holy Place—the very presence of an infinitely holy God (Hebrews 10:10). It is the blood of Christ, according to the Romans passage we have been examining, that turns the holy and just wrath of God away from us.

Therefore when we are smarting under the conviction of sin, when we realize we've failed God one more time, perhaps even in the same sin, we must resort to the cleansing blood of Jesus. As a well-known gospel hymn from the nineteenth century expressed it,

> What can wash away my sin?
> Nothing but the blood of Jesus;
> What can make me whole again?
> Nothing but the blood of Jesus.[7]

It is not our contrition or sorrow for our sin, it is not our repentance, it is not even the passing of a certain number of hours during which we feel we are on some kind of probation that cleanses us. It is the blood of Christ, shed once for all on Calvary two thousand years ago but appropriated daily or even many times a day, that cleanses our consciences and gives us a renewed sense of peace with God.

PREACH THE GOSPEL TO YOURSELF

This then is the gospel with which we need to become thoroughly familiar and that we need to preach to ourselves every day. Jesus by His death and shed blood completely satisfied the justice of God and the claims of His broken law. By His perfect obedience He positively fulfilled the requirements of the law. Thus in both its precepts and penalty, the law of God in its most exacting requirements was fulfilled by Jesus. And He did this in our place as our representative and our substitute.

To preach the gospel to yourself, then, means that you continually face up to your own sinfulness and then flee to Jesus through faith in His shed blood and righteous life. It means that you appropriate, again by faith, the fact that Jesus fully satisfied the law of God, that He is your propitiation, and that God's holy wrath is no longer directed toward you.

To preach the gospel to yourself means that you take at face value the precious words of Romans 4:7-8—

> Blessed are they
> > whose transgressions are forgiven,
> > whose sins are covered.
> Blessed is the man
> > whose sin the Lord will never count against him.

It means that you believe on the testimony of God that "Therefore, there is now no condemnation for those who are in Christ Jesus" (Romans 8:1). It means you believe that "Christ redeemed [you] from the curse of the law by becoming a curse for [you], for it is written: 'Cursed is everyone who is hung on a tree'" (Galatians 3:13). It means you believe He forgave you all your sins (Colossians 2:13) and now "[presents you] holy in his sight, without blemish and free from accusation" (Colossians 1:22).

Turning to the Old Testament, to preach the gospel to yourself means that you appropriate by faith the words of Isaiah 53:6—

We all, like sheep, have gone astray,
    each of us has turned to his own way;
and the LORD has laid on him
    the iniquity of us all.

It means that you dwell upon the promise that God has removed your transgressions from you as far as the east is from the west (Psalm 103:12), that He has blotted out your transgressions and remembers your sin no more (Isaiah 43:25). (See also Isaiah 38:17 and Micah 7:19 for other assurances of God's forgiveness.) But it means you realize that all these wonderful promises of forgiveness are based upon the atoning death of Jesus Christ.

It is the death of Christ through which He satisfied the justice of God and averted from us the wrath of God that is the basis of all God's promises of forgiveness. We must be careful that, in preaching the gospel to ourselves, we do not preach a gospel without a cross. We must be careful that we do not rely on the so-called unconditional love of God without realizing that His love can only flow to us as a result of Christ's atoning death.

This is the gospel by which we were saved, and it is the gospel by which we must live every day of our Christian lives. In Romans 3:24, Paul said we are justified by grace, referring to what we might call our point-in-time salvation, the day we trusted in Christ. In Romans 5:2, however, Paul spoke of "this grace in which we now stand." Here he refers to our day-to-day standing before God as being on the same basis as our justification—that is, on the basis of grace. But this grace—unmerited favor to those who deserve wrath—comes to us through the Lord Jesus Christ.

God is the "God of all grace" (1 Peter 5:10) and is disposed to deal with us by grace, but not at the expense of His justice. But with justice satisfied, God can now deal with us in grace, both in our salvation and in our day-to-day relationship with Him.

This is a book about God's grace and the pursuit of

holiness. You can be sure of one thing, though: When you set yourself to seriously pursue holiness, you will begin to realize what an awful sinner you are. And if you are not firmly rooted in the gospel and have not learned to preach it to yourself every day, you will soon become discouraged and will slack off in your pursuit of holiness.

We will consider a number of factors that go into the pursuit of holiness in later chapters of this book. But none is more important than learning to preach the gospel to yourself every day.

OTHER REFERENCES:
    Rom 5:12 – 6:4

4

WE DIED TO SIN

What shall we say, then?
Shall we go on sinning so that grace may increase?
By no means! We died to sin;
how can we live in it any longer?
ROMANS 6:1-2

WE HAVE SEEN THAT the gospel is the good news that Christ died in our place to pay the penalty for our sins. As a result we are declared "not guilty" in the court of Heaven. Not only that, we are also declared "righteous" in God's sight because the perfect righteousness of Jesus Christ has been credited to all who have trusted in Him.

There is still more good news. The death of Christ secured for us not only freedom from the penalty of sin, but also deliverance from the dominion of sin in our lives. I realize that statement may sound unbelievable to some who are struggling with one or more sinful habits, but it is indeed true. In this chapter we will see how that is true; that is, in what way God has delivered us from the dominion of sin, and how we work out that truth in our daily lives.

Just as Romans 3:19-26 is the classic passage of Scripture about salvation from the penalty of sin, so Romans 6:1-14 is the primary passage of Scripture about freedom from the dominion of sin. In this section of Scripture we learn what

God has done for us through Christ to enable us to deal with sin, even persistent sin, in our lives. We will see in Romans 6 that the gospel is far more than "fire insurance" from eternal punishment in hell. We will learn that through Christ's death on the cross, we are given the ability to live lives that are both pleasing to God and fulfilling for ourselves.

I must warn you beforehand, however, that in learning how God has delivered us from the dominion of sin, we are going to wrestle with some of the Apostle Paul's most difficult-to-understand teaching. Don't think of this section of Scripture, however, as "just doctrine," as a mere theoretical or intellectual exercise. Romans 6:1-14 has some very practical applications for us that are essential to the pursuit of holiness. So as you read this chapter, be prepared to think, and try to stay with me as we explore these wonderful truths together.

SHALL WE GO ON SINNING?

Romans 6:1-2, the epigraph for this chapter, is an introduction to the subject of sanctification. Paul had in Romans 5:20 asserted that "where sin increased, grace increased all the more." In making such an almost grandiose statement about God's grace, Paul anticipated the objection expressed in Romans 6:1—"Shall we go on sinning so that grace may increase?"

This question can arise from either of two sources. It can arise from people who see God's grace and the total forgiveness of our sins as an open door to irresponsible, sinful behavior based on the notion that "If God loves me unconditionally regardless of my behavior, then I'm free to live as I please." Or the question can arise from concerned Christians who are fearful that a strong emphasis on God's grace will indeed lead people to live such irresponsible lives. It seems that whenever the gospel is preached in all its fullness, the objection is inevitably raised that such a message of free and total forgiveness through Christ will cause Christians to treat sin lightly.

Paul deals with this issue and answers the objection. In

doing so, however, he moves into the more positive teaching of the believer's freedom from the dominion of sin. The reason he can do this so easily is that both the answer to the objection and our freedom from sin's dominion are bound up in one great New Testament truth—the believer's union with Christ. We are going to explore this concept more in this chapter, but for now let's look at Paul's response to the question of believers continuing in sin.

To do this, let us notice, first, the context of the question. The greater context is Paul's exposition of the gospel beginning in Romans 3:21 and culminating in that glorious statement in 5:20, "But where sin increased, grace increased all the more." As I have already indicated, it is that seemingly unguarded statement that gives rise to the troublesome thought, "Shall we go on sinning so that grace may increase?"

The more immediate context is Paul's explanation of the representative character of both Adam and Christ and the results of their respective actions on their peoples (Romans 5:12-21). The proper understanding of Paul's response in Romans 6 must be based on what he taught in 5:12-21. So we will return to this passage a little later. But for now, let's see how Paul handled the objection that overflowing grace in the presence of sin might well lead to more sin.

First, note that Paul did not back down. He didn't say, "Oh, you misunderstood what I meant. I didn't intend to say that God's grace was so unqualified." Neither did he say, as we will see in studying his response, "How could you possibly think such a thing or act in that way? That would be the height of ingratitude to God for His grace."

Paul's response was, "By no means! We died to sin; how can we live in it any longer?" (Romans 6:2). Paul's answer to the objection is not, "How could you think such a thing?" but rather, it is impossible by the nature of the case for such to happen.

What is the nature of the case that makes continuing in a life of sin impossible? The answer is, we died to sin. Paul's "we died to sin" has been a difficult and often misunderstood expression. We must, however, determine Paul's meaning if we are to properly understand his response to the objection that the preaching of grace may well lead to increased sinful behavior.

The first thing we note about Paul's statement that we died to sin is that this death has already occurred in the past. It is not something we should do but something we have already done. Every person in this world who is a true believer has died to sin. We are not to "die more and more unto sin." We cannot possibly die to sin any more than we have. In chapter 11 we will talk about putting sin to death (Romans 8:13), but that action is altogether different from the death to sin Paul was talking about here.

A second observation on the fact that all believers have died to sin is that this death occurred even though the believer may not be aware of it. Our awareness or understanding of a fact like this does not make it any more true, but it does determine how we respond to and apply the fact. It *is* important that we understand in what sense we died to sin, because, as we will see beginning in verse 11, Paul did intend that we apply the truth to our lives. But again, our death to sin is an objective fact, not dependent on our awareness or understanding to make it true.

The third thing to note is that we died to sin through our union with Christ. Observe how Paul kept repeating that idea in the following verses: We were baptized into His death (verse 3); we were buried with Him (verse 4); we have been united with Him in His death (verse 5); our old self was crucified with Him (verse 6); and we died with Christ (verse 8). Note that in verse 10 Paul said Christ died to sin, whereas in verse 8 he said we died with Christ. That is why Paul could say in verse 2 that we died to sin. When Christ died to sin, we died to sin also.

We still have not answered the question, "What does it mean to die to sin?" To arrive at the answer, we must first pursue what the expression "union with Christ" means. In exploring this term we will discover that union with Christ involves far more than dying to sin, but that death to sin is one of its more fundamental results.

UNION WITH CHRIST

The New Testament concept of the believer's union with Christ is one of the most important truths of Scripture. Scottish theologian Sinclair Ferguson says it is "a doctrine which lies at the heart of the Christian life" and "the truth to which the New Testament constantly returns."[1] As I indicated in chapter 3 (page 53), it is the basis of our justification and, as we will see in this chapter, also the basis of our sanctification.

The concept of the believer's union with Christ is especially important in the teaching of Paul. His usual "shorthand" expressions for union with Christ are "in Christ," "in Him," and "in the Lord." British author John Stott says those three expressions occur no less than 164 times in Paul's letters.[2] For our purposes of answering the concern that too much emphasis on God's grace may lead to irresponsible, sinful behavior, the doctrine of the believer's union with Christ is the basis upon which Paul refuted that charge in Romans 6.

Historically, Bible commentators and expositors have considered the believer's union with Christ as having two different aspects, bringing about two different results. The first is called a representative union, or what some theologians and commentators call a federal union. The second is called a vital or spiritual union.[3]

REPRESENTATIVE UNION

The classic passage of Scripture on the representative union of Christ and His people is Romans 5:12-21. Though Paul's presentation is somewhat difficult to follow, it can be summed up in what he said in 1 Corinthians 15:22—"For as in Adam all die, so in Christ all will be made alive." Even this scripture can be misunderstood unless we realize that the two "alls" in the verse are not equal in meaning. Evangelical Bible commentators agree that the two "alls" mean, respectively, all who are in Adam, and all who are in Christ, in both cases by virtue of this representative or federal union. This union may be depicted by two circles representing, respectively, Adam and Christ as seen in the following illustration.

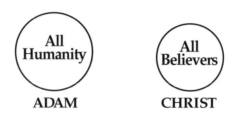

Every human being (except Christ) was born into the circle of Adam. Every person who trusts in Jesus Christ as Savior is born into the circle of Christ. Note that the circle representing Christ is smaller than the one representing Adam, because only those who trust in Christ are in Him.

What Paul taught in Romans 5:12-21 is first, that all human beings (except Jesus) sinned in Adam as their federal representative. As a result, all of us experience death, which is the consequence of sin (verse 12). Because of Adam's representative capacity, his sin was as truly our sin as if it had been committed by each one of us. It is only in this way that all of us could be involved in its consequences. This concept is called the federal headship of Adam.

This federal headship or representative capacity is somewhat illustrated by the concept of power of attorney. A friend of mine wanted to refinance the mortgage on his house to take advantage of lower interest rates. When the date for the closing was finally set, he realized he and his wife would be out of the country at that time. He asked if I would represent them at the closing, and I agreed, so he and his wife executed a power of attorney authorizing me to act on their behalf.

I went to the closing and, as my friends' legal representative, signed all kinds of papers. When I signed those documents it was just as if they had signed them. When I signed the promissory note to pay a certain amount each month, that act was as legally binding on them as if they had signed the note, because I was acting as their legal representative. In like manner, Adam was our legal representative in the garden, and when he sinned, his action was as binding on us as if we had sinned personally.

We may object that we did not appoint Adam as our representative in the garden. To do so is futile, however, for in our objection we are actually complaining against God. It should be enough for us to know that God, the Sovereign Creator of the universe and the One in whom we live, and move, and have our being, appointed him.

The really good news, however, and the main point Paul was driving home is that just as Adam was our federal representative in his sin, so Jesus Christ was our federal representative in His sinless life and atoning death. Therefore, just as Adam's sin brought condemnation and death to all his race, that is, all human beings except Christ, so our Lord's act of righteousness brought justification and life to all His race, that is, all who trust in Him (verses 18-19).

Because of this representative union between Christ and His people, all of our responsibilities before God rest upon Him, and all of His merit accrues to us. Jesus, as our representative, assumed all the obligations in which Adam failed, and fulfilled them on our behalf. So, just as Adam's sin was as truly our sin as if we had committed it, so Christ's perfect obedience to God's law and His death to pay the penalty of a broken law are just as much our obedience and death as if we had perfectly obeyed God's law and died on that cross.

As George Smeaton so helpfully wrote, "We have but one public representative, corporate act performed by the Son of God, in which we share as truly as if we had accomplished that atonement ourselves."[4] So, as Dr. Smeaton again wrote, "Thus we may either say, Christ died for us; or say, we died in Him. We may equally affirm He was crucified for us, or we were co-crucified with Him."[5] The latter expression is in fact what Paul essentially said when he wrote, "I have been crucified with Christ" (Galatians 2:20).

All this discussion of Christ's federal representation on behalf of His people may seem like needless theological fine print to some people, but in reality it is one of the most exciting teachings of Scripture. I have been asserting from the very beginning of this book that our day-to-day standing before God, as well as our eternal destiny, is based not on our performance but upon our Lord's performance. The only truth that makes that argument valid is that Jesus "performed" as our legal representative.

Therefore when our consciences condemn us for our sins or our failures to fulfill the disciplines of the Christian life, we must go back to the fact that Jesus is our legal representative and that in that capacity He perfectly obeyed the will of His Father. He could rightfully say, "I always do what pleases him" (John 8:29), and when He pleased the Father, we pleased the Father. Our entire confidence in our acceptance before God is based solely upon the fact that Jesus was our legal representative in His sinless life and obedient death.

When I think deeply on this truth and its implications on my relationship with a Holy God, I get very excited. On several occasions when Paul had written on some profound truth, he spontaneously broke out into a doxology of praise to God. Words flowed from his heart, such as,

> Oh, the depth of the riches of the wisdom and knowledge of God!
> How unsearchable his judgments,
> and his paths beyond tracing out! (Romans 11:33)

> Now to the King eternal, immortal, invisible, the only God, be honor and glory for ever and ever.
> (1 Timothy 1:17)

That is the way I feel in my heart right now as I write about the wonderful truth that through our union with Him, Jesus represented us before God in His life and death.

SIN'S REIGN AND DOMINION

All I have said about our union with Christ in His death may seem like a digression, but it is necessary in order for us to finally address what Paul meant when he said we died to sin. To answer the question, we need to go back to his statement in Romans 5:21, that "sin reigned in death." Sin is personified by Paul and viewed by him as reigning over us in a kingdom of death. Why did sin reign? The answer is because of our guilt in Adam. The penal consequence of our guilt was to be delivered over unto sin as a *legal* reign, and the result of that was to be brought under the dominion of sin. The penal reign of sin and its corrupting dominion in our lives are inseparable and equal in extent.

David spoke of this legal reign and consequent dominion of sin in our lives when he said,

> Surely I was sinful at birth,
>   sinful from the time my mother conceived me.
> (Psalm 51:5)

The only reason David would say he was sinful at birth, before he had actually committed any sin, was because he realized he was born under Adam's guilt and so experienced the dominion of sin in his life.

To die to sin then means, first of all, to die to its legal or penal reign and, secondly, as a necessary result, to die to its dominion over us. We speak of the total depravity of a person who is outside of Christ. We do not mean the person is as wicked as he or she can possibly be, but that sin has corrupted the person's entire being. Guilt, and its penal consequence, is the source and ongoing cause of this depravity. Therefore, deliverance from guilt and its penal consequences brings deliverance from sin's dominion. In God's plan of salvation these two deliverances are necessarily connected. There is no such thing as salvation from sin's penalty without an accompanying deliverance from sin's dominion. This obviously does not mean we no longer sin, but that sin no longer *reigns* in our lives.

How did we die to sin? We have already noted that we died to sin through our union with Christ. Paul said in Romans 6:10 that Christ died to sin, and in verse 8 he said we died with Christ. That Christ died to sin is a rather startling but wonderful statement. Christ did not die to the *dominion* of sin, as He was never under it. However, when He was made sin for us (2 Corinthians 5:21)—that is, when He was charged with our sin—He did come under its legal reign and was made subject to its penalty.

When Jesus died, He died to the legal reign of sin. Through our federal union with Him in His death, we, too, died to the legal reign of sin. But since the legal reign and the practical dominion of sin in our lives are inseparable, we died not only to its legal reign but also to its corrupting dominion over us. Hallelujah! What a Savior we have who was able to not only free us from sin's penalty but also from its dominion.

The question arises, however, "If we died to sin's dominion, why do we still struggle with sins in our daily lives?" When Paul wrote, "We died to sin; how can we live in it any longer?" he was referring, not to the activity of committing sins, but to continuing to live under the dominion of sin. The word *live* means to continue in or abide in. It connotes a settled course of life. To use Paul's words from Romans 8:7, "The sinful mind [one under sin's dominion] is hostile to God. It does not submit to God's law, nor can it do so." But the believer who has died to sin's reign and dominion delights in God's law. The believer approves of it as holy, righteous, and good (Romans 7:12), even though he or she may struggle to obey it.

We must distinguish between the activity of sin, which is true in all believers, and the dominion of sin, which is true of all unbelievers. Sinclair Ferguson has written, "Sin is not primarily an activity of man's will so much as a captivity which man suffers, as an alien *power* grips his soul. It is an axiom for [John] Owen [whose teaching Ferguson is summarizing] that while the *presence* of sin can never be abolished in this life, nor the *influence* of sin altered (its tendency is always the same), its *dominion* can, indeed, must be destroyed if a man is to be a Christian."[6]

Therefore a believer cannot continue in sin. We no longer live in the realm of sin, under its reign and practical dominion. We have, to use Paul's words, died to sin. We indeed do sin and even our best deeds are stained with sin, but our attitude toward it is essentially different from that of an unbeliever. We succumb to temptations, either from our own evil desires (James 1:13), or from the world or the Devil (Ephesians 2:1-3), but this is different from a settled disposition. Further, to paraphrase from Ferguson on John Owen, our sin is a burden that afflicts us rather than a pleasure that delights us.

The late Scottish theologian John Murray wrote on Romans 6:2, "What the apostle has in view is the once-for-all definitive breach with sin which constitutes the identity of the believer. A believer cannot therefore live in sin; if a man lives in sin he is not a believer. If we view sin as a realm or sphere then the believer no longer lives in that realm or sphere."[7]

My perception of present-day Christendom is that most believers have little understanding of what Dr. Murray calls the "once-for-all definitive breach with sin." But it is this decisive deliverance from the dominion of sin through union with Christ in His death that ensures that a true believer will not have the cavalier attitude, "Shall we go on sinning so that grace may increase?" If a person does have such an attitude, it is a likely indication that the person is not a true believer, however much he or she professes to have trusted in Christ for salvation.

ALIVE TO GOD

There is yet another reason why Paul is confident that the preaching of the gospel of grace will not result in irresponsible living. Not only are we dead to sin, we are also alive to God in Christ Jesus (Romans 6:11). Not only does sin no longer reign in death over us, now grace reigns through righteousness (Romans 5:21). Not only have we been rescued from the dominion of darkness, we have been brought into the kingdom of God's dear Son (Colossians 1:13).

What does it mean to be alive unto God? Earlier in this chapter I mentioned the two different aspects of our union with Christ: the federal or legal union, and the vital or spiritual union. So far we have looked at our legal union with Christ in His death and how that has freed us from the legal reign and consequent corrupting dominion of sin. But as we consider what it means to be alive unto God, we enter into the sphere of the vital or spiritual union.

The vital union is a spiritually organic union of the believer with Jesus Christ. By organic I refer to a living union. Jesus Himself gave us the best illustration of this organic union when He gave us the vine-and-branches illustration in John 15:1-5. It is quite obvious that the branches are joined to the vine by an organic or living union as opposed to simply being attached to the vine in some dead, mechanical fashion. In the same way, believers are united to Christ in such a way that, in the words of the Apostle Peter, we "participate in the divine nature" (2 Peter 1:4). That is, just as the branches share in the life of the vine, so we share in the very life of Christ Himself. That is why being "in Christ" was so important to Paul. It was not just a theological concept to him. It was the very essence of his Christian life. It was much more than a close relationship such as two friends might have. It was his very life. Paul lived as a branch participating in the life of the vine. He lived every day as a person "in Christ."

Not only are we in Christ, He is also in us (Galatians 2:20, Ephesians 3:17). Christ enters into our humanity through the indwelling of His Holy Spirit to renew us and to transform us more and more into His likeness. This presence of Christ within us to make us holy is another assurance that we as believers cannot continue in a life of sin or have a continued cavalier attitude toward sin. We will study our dependence on Christ in chapter 8. This dependence, however, is not like the dependence of a child on his or her father for support. The child is not "in" the father. Our dependence is like the dependence of the branches on the vine for both life and nourishment.

Our union with Christ is not only organic or living; it is a spiritual as opposed to a physical union. We need to keep in mind, however, that the spiritual dimension is just as real as the physical dimension. The fact that the spiritual dimension of our lives cannot be seen does not make it any less real. We really are participants in the very life of Christ. He really does dwell in us by His Spirit.

We should also note that the legal union discussed earlier in this chapter secures for us the vital union. Christ's death to sin and His satisfaction of God's justice opened the way for the reign of grace in our lives.

Paul opened Romans 6 with a resounding refutation of the notion that the gospel promotes irresponsible, sinful behavior. He showed not only that it does not, but that it is the very nature of the gospel to ensure that such a thing cannot happen. In addressing this issue, Paul very naturally transitioned from justification to sanctification, or the pursuit of holiness. We will begin to address the practical aspects of sanctification in the next chapter, but for now, I want to call our attention to the grace of God in sanctification.

All Christians believe that we are saved by grace (Ephesians 2:8). But we have seen in this chapter that salvation includes both deliverance from the penalty of sin and freedom from the dominion of sin. We have seen that our legal union with Christ in His death and resurrection secures our vital union with Him by which we participate in His divine nature. It is through this vital union that we receive the enabling power to live the Christian life.

Please note that all this is from God. Deliverance from both the penalty and the dominion of sin is by His grace. We could not take one step in the pursuit of holiness if God in His grace had not first delivered us from the dominion of sin and brought us into union with His risen Son. Salvation is by grace and sanctification is by grace.

DO NOT LET SIN REIGN

Paul sometimes uses the same expression in both the indicative (a statement of fact) and imperative (a statement of command) moods.[8] For example, in Galatians 3:27 he said, "For all of you who were baptized into Christ have clothed yourselves with Christ" (an indicative statement). However, in Romans 13:14, he exhorted us to "clothe [ourselves] with the Lord Jesus Christ" (an imperative command). Similarly, on many occasions he spoke of us as being "in Christ Jesus" (for example, 1 Corinthians 1:30, 2 Corinthians 5:17), all of these being indicative statements. Yet in Colossians 2:6, he exhorted us to "continue to live in him," an imperative exhortation.

We find another illustration of this in Romans 6:11-13. Paul had just explained in rather elaborate fashion that believers have died to the reign of sin. But in verse 12 he exhorted us not to let sin reign in our mortal bodies. "Why," we may ask, "if we died to the reign of sin, do we need to be exhorted not to let sin reign in our bodies?" Basically Paul was saying in this and the above instances, "Live out in your lives the reality of the gospel. Take advantage of and put to use all the provisions of grace God has given you in Christ."

John Murray has given us an excellent illustration of the relationship of the imperative to the indicative. He wrote, "To say to the slave who has not been emancipated, 'Do not behave as a slave' is to mock his enslavement. But to say the same to the slave who has been set free is the necessary appeal to put into effect the privileges and rights of his liberation."[9]

We will consider the imperatives of Romans 6:12-13 in later chapters. For now, however, we want to look at verse 11, which says, "In the same way, count yourselves dead to sin but alive to God in Christ Jesus." Actually verse 11 is an imperative, but it is an exhortation to *believe* something, not to *do* something. We are to count on or believe the fact that we actually did die to the guilt and consequent dominion of sin. To borrow from Professor Murray's slave illustration, we are to believe that we truly have been set free. Not only are we to believe we have died to sin; we are also to believe we are alive unto God, united to the risen Christ, and partakers of His divine nature. It is the belief of this truth that will give us the courage not to let sin reign in our mortal bodies. And it is through reliance upon this truth that we will experience the power of His Spirit, who dwells within us to enable us to resist the motions of sin so that it is not able to reign in us.

During the long years of the Cold War between the United States and the Soviet Union, a Russian air force pilot flew his fighter plane from a base in Russia to an American air force base in Japan and asked for asylum. He was flown to the United States where he was duly debriefed, given a new identity, and set up as a bona fide resident of the United States. In due time he became an American citizen.

The Russian pilot's experience illustrates to some degree what happened to us when we died to sin and were made alive to God. He changed kingdoms; he was given a new identity and a new status. He was no longer a Russian; he was now an American. He was no longer under the rule of what was then an oppressive and totalitarian government. Now he was free to experience all of the advantages and resources of living in a free and prosperous country.

This former Russian pilot, however, was still the same person. He had the same personality, the same habits, and the same cultural patterns as he did before he flew out of Russia. But he did have a new identity and a new status. As a result of his new identity and status as a citizen in a free country, he now had the opportunity to grow as a free person, to discard the mind-set of someone living under bondage, and to put off the habit patterns of a person living under the heel of a despotic regime. Furthermore, as a benefactor of our government's intelligence establishment, he was furnished all the resources needed to make a successful transition to an American citizen.

In effect, this Russian pilot "died" to his old identity as a Russian citizen and was "made alive" in a new identity as an American citizen. As an American, all the resources of our government were at his disposal to become in fact what he had become in status. But this could not have happened without first changing his status.

When we as believers died to sin, we died to a status wherein we were under bondage to the tyrannical reign of sin. At the same time we were granted citizenship in the Kingdom of God and, through our vital union with Jesus Christ, were furnished all the resources we need to become in fact what we have become in status. We have been given all we need to bring the imperative—"do not let sin reign in your mortal body"—into line with the indicative—"we died to sin." But this could not have happened without a change in our status. And it is through our legal union with Christ in His death and resurrection that our status has been forever changed.

We must count on this and believe it. We must by faith in God's Word lay hold on the fact that we have died to the reign of sin and are now alive to God, under His reign of grace. Unless we do this we will find ourselves seeking to pursue holiness by the strength of our own wills, not by the grace of God.

So the imperative to pursue holiness—to not let sin reign in our mortal bodies—is based on the fact of grace. That is, through our union with Christ in His death to sin and life to God, God has given us all the resources we need to pursue holiness.

Therefore, we can say the truth that "where sin increased, grace increased all the more" (Romans 5:20), far from being an occasion to sin all the more, is actually the only provision from God whereby we can deal with sin and make any progress in the pursuit of holiness. That is why I said early in chapter 1 that the pursuit of holiness, while requiring all-out effort on our part, must be firmly anchored in the grace of God.

5

DISCIPLINED BY GRACE

For the grace of God that brings salvation has appeared to all men. It teaches us to say "No" to ungodliness and worldly passions, and to live self-controlled, upright and godly lives in this present age.

TITUS 2:11-12

I ENJOY OXYMORA, THOSE often-humorous, contradictory expressions such as "Hotpoint refrigerators" or Yogi Berra's observation about the shadows in Yankee Stadium's outfield, "It gets late early out here." But the classic for me is a couple of lines from a Boy Scout camp song we used to sing, "O Susanna," which went,

It rained all night the day I left;
The weather it was dry.
The sun was so hot I froze to death,
Susanna, don't you cry.

The title of this chapter may seem to some people like an oxymoron. Discipline, to them, suggests restraint and legalism, rules and regulations, and a God who frowns on anyone who has fun. Grace, on the other hand, seems to mean freedom from any rules, spontaneous and unstructured living, and most of all, a God who loves us unconditionally regardless of our sinful behavior.

Such thinking reflects a misunderstanding of both grace and discipline. In fact, as we can see from the epigraph of this chapter, the same grace that brings salvation to us also disciplines us as believers. The verse actually reads, "the grace of God . . . *teaches* us." The word translated as "teach," however, means much more than the usual idea we assign to it of imparting knowledge. Originally it was used as a term for the rearing of children and included not only instruction, but also admonition, reproof, and punishment, all administered in love and for the benefit of the child. The Apostle Paul used the same word in Ephesians 6:4 when he charged fathers to bring up their children in the training (that is, discipline) and instruction of the Lord.

Used in a spiritual sense, discipline includes all instruction, all reproof and correction, and all providentially directed hardships in our lives that are aimed at cultivating spiritual growth and godly character. And though in the physical realm children eventually reach adulthood and are no longer under the discipline of their parents, in the spiritual realm we remain under God's parental discipline as long as we live.

So we see that the very same grace that brings salvation also trains us to live lives that are pleasing to God. All of God's disciplinary processes are grounded in His grace— His unmerited and unconditional favor toward us. We tend to equate discipline with rules and performance standards; God equates it with firm but loving care for our souls.

When I was first introduced to the idea of Christian discipleship, I was given a list of seven spiritual disciplines I should practice every day—things such as a daily quiet time, Bible study, Scripture memorization, and prayer. All of those disciplines were very helpful to me, and I am grateful for every one of them. They formed the foundation for my spiritual growth.

However, while learning those disciplines I came to believe that my day-to-day relationship with God depended on how faithfully I performed them. No one actually told me that God's approval of me was based on my performance. Still, I developed a vague but real impression that God's smile or frown depended on whether or not I did my spiritual exercises. The challenge to be faithful in my quiet time, while good in itself, probably contributed to this impression.

My experience is not unusual. A friend of mine who ministers on a university campus told of a student who was exceptionally diligent in having his daily quiet time. My friend asked the student why he was so rigid in his practice, and the young man responded, "So nothing bad will happen to me." He was not being disciplined by grace but by legalism.

We are performance-oriented by nature, and our culture, and sometimes our upbringing, reinforces this legalistic mind-set. All too often a child's acceptance by his or her parents is based on the child's performance, and this certainly tends to be true in our society. We carry this same type of thinking into our relationship with God. So, whether it is our response to God's discipline of us or our practice of those spiritual disciplines that are so good and helpful, we tend to think it is the "law" of God rather than the grace of God that disciplines us.

Paul said, though, that it is the very same grace—God's unmerited favor—that brought salvation to us in the first place that disciplines us. This means that all our responses to God's dealings with us and all our practice of the spiritual disciplines must be based on the knowledge that God is dealing with us in grace. And it means that all our effort to teach godly living and spiritual maturity to others must be grounded in grace. If we fail to teach that discipline is by grace, people will assume, as I did, that it is by performance.

That is why we must not put the gospel on the shelf once a person becomes a new believer. He or she will have just as difficult a time believing that God relates to us every day on the basis of grace as a person has believing that God saves by grace instead of by works. So we must not only preach the gospel to ourselves every day, we must continue to teach it and preach it to those whom we may be discipling in some way, whether in a Sunday school class or Bible study we are teaching or in a one-to-one mentoring relationship. Discipleship must be based on God's grace.

SALVATION AND DISCIPLINE ARE INSEPARABLE

Another truth we see in Titus 2:11-12 is that salvation and spiritual discipline are inseparable. The grace that brings salvation to us also disciplines us. It does not do the one without the other. That is, God never saves people and leaves them alone to continue in their immaturity and sinful lifestyle. Those whom He saves, He disciplines. Paul said this another way in Philippians 1:6—"He who began a good work in you will carry it on to completion until the day of Christ Jesus."

This thought is both encouraging and sobering. It is encouraging because it assures us that our spiritual growth is not left to our initiative, nor is it dependent upon our wisdom to know in which areas and in which direction we need to grow. Rather, it is God Himself who initiates and superintends our spiritual growth. This is not to say that we have no responsibility to respond to God's spiritual child-training in our lives, but it is to say that He is the one in charge of our training.

Of course, God will use others, such as our pastors and other mature Christians, as His agents, and He will use various means, primarily His Word and circumstances, to discipline us, but He is the one who takes the ultimate responsibility. And as the one who is infinite in wisdom, He knows exactly which means to use in our lives at any given time. Our response then should be to trust Him and obey Him, and, to use words from the writer of Hebrews, to pray that He will "work in us what is pleasing to him" (13:21).

At the same time this inseparability of God's grace and spiritual discipline is a sobering truth. One has only to look around at Christendom, particularly in the United States, to see that there is a vast multitude of people who claim to have trusted in Christ at some time but do not seem to have experienced any of the discipline of grace. They may have walked an aisle, signed a card, or even prayed a prayer, but grace is not teaching them to say no to ungodliness and worldly passions, let alone to live self-controlled, upright, and godly lives. Essentially, their lives are no different today than they were before they professed to have trusted Christ.

As I think of these people, I am reminded of the words of Hebrews 12:8, "If you are not disciplined (and everyone undergoes discipline), then you are illegitimate children and not true sons." And Jesus Himself said, "Not everyone who says to me, 'Lord, Lord,' will enter the kingdom of heaven, but only he who does the will of my Father who is in heaven" (Matthew 7:21). It is not those who have merely made a profession, but those in whose lives there is evidence of God's Fatherly child-training, who are the inheritors of eternal life.

This sobering truth should be reflected upon by each of us. Is God's grace disciplining me? The Apostle Paul said, "Examine yourselves to see whether you are in the faith; test yourselves. Do you not realize that Christ Jesus is in you—unless, of course, you fail the test?" (2 Corinthians 13:5). And the Apostle Peter exhorted us to "be all the more eager to make [our] calling and election sure" (2 Peter 1:10). Are you truly trusting in Jesus Christ as your Savior as He is presented in the gospel that we studied in chapter 3? Is there any evidence that you have died to the reign of sin through union with Jesus Christ? And is the grace of God at work in you to discipline or train you so that you are growing spiritually? If your honest answer is "no," I urge you to come to Him believing His words that "whoever comes to me I will never drive away" (John 6:37).

Let me be clear at this point. We do not pursue holiness or the evidences of God's discipline to attain salvation. That would be salvation by works. Rather, God's discipline in our lives, and the desire to pursue holiness on our part, be it ever so faint, is the inevitable result of receiving God's gift of salvation by faith. As Martin Luther is so often quoted as saying, "We are saved by faith alone, but the faith that saves is never alone."

Many of us have friends and relatives who profess to be Christians but in whose lives there appears to be no evidence of the discipline of grace. Oftentimes we cling to a frail hope that such persons are believers because they made a profession at some time, despite the lack of any evidence of the Spirit's work in their lives. It seems parents are especially prone to this form of denial regarding children who show no evidence of a genuine work of grace.

We certainly cannot determine the reality of another person's salvation, and we can never say a certain individual is not a Christian. Nevertheless, we should not be naive in the face of a lack of evidence of any spiritual life. Instead of clinging to what may well be a false hope, we should pray earnestly that God will bring that person to salvation, or if perchance He has, will begin to manifest the discipline of grace in the person's life.

GRACE TEACHES US TO SAY NO

Still another truth we see in Titus 2:11-12 is that the discipline that grace administers to us has both a negative and a positive aspect. This should not surprise us when we think of discipline as child-training. Every responsible parent not only wants to deal with misbehavior in a child but also desires to promote positive character traits. Both are necessary in physical child-training, and both are necessary in the spiritual realm.

Grace first teaches us to say no to ungodliness and worldly passions. Ungodliness is usually equated with wickedness: that which is immoral, dishonest, cruel, evil, or debased (see, for example, Romans 1:18-32). Ungodliness, however, in its broadest form basically comprises disregarding God, ignoring Him, or not taking Him into account in one's life. It is a lack of fear and reverence for Him. The wickedness portrayed by Paul in Romans 1:18-32 all starts with the idea that "although they knew God, they neither glorified him as God nor gave thanks to him" (verse 21). In this wider sense, then, a person may be highly moral and even benevolent and still be ungodly.

I recently read a review of a book titled *Timelines of the Ancient World*, published by the Smithsonian Institution. The reviewer pointed out that even though great figures of history such as Alexander the Great are duly mentioned, not one word is said about the great men of the Bible such as Moses, Abraham, or David. Most revealing of all is the fact that not so much as a passing reference is made to Jesus Christ, despite the fact that the book uses the BC and AD suffixes in its dating. The editors unwittingly testified to the historical reality of Him around whom time is measured without even mentioning His name.

I suspect the Smithsonian editors are nice, decent people, the kind you would enjoy having as your neighbor. But if their book is an indicator, they are ungodly people. They have no regard for God.

When we trust in Christ as our Savior, we bring a *habit* of ungodliness into our Christian lives. Like the Smithsonian editors, we were accustomed to living without regard for God. As unbelievers, we cared neither for His glory nor His will. Basically, we ignored Him. But now that we have been delivered from the dominion of sin and brought under the reign of grace, grace teaches us to renounce this attitude (as well as actions) of ungodliness. Obviously this training does not occur all at once. In fact, God will be rooting out ungodliness from our lives as long as we live on this earth.

Grace also teaches us to say no to worldly passions, the inordinate desire for and preoccupation with the things of this life, such as possessions, prestige, pleasure, or power. Worldly passion is the opposite of the attitude Paul urged on us when he wrote, "Those who use the things of the world, [should live] as if not engrossed in them. For this world in its present form is passing away" (1 Corinthians 7:31).

What does it mean to say no to ungodliness and worldly

passions? Basically it means a decisive break with those attitudes and practices. In one sense this decisive break is a divine act that occurred when we died to the dominion of sin in our lives. In fact, the tense of the Greek denotes the thought of *having denied* ungodliness and worldly passions, a prior act. In another sense, however, we are to work out this breach with sin by putting to death the misdeeds of the body (Romans 8:13). We will develop this idea further in chapter 11. But for now, to say no to worldly passions means "to abstain from sinful desires, which war against your soul" (1 Peter 2:11). It means that we recognize these desires as "deceitful" (Ephesians 4:22) and "evil" (James 1:14), and thus refuse the pleasure they suggest and the acts to which they beckon us.

GRACE TEACHES US TO SAY YES

Sometimes we can get the impression that the Christian life consists mainly of a series of negative prohibitions: "Do not do this" and "Do not do that." Prohibitions are definitely an important part of our spiritual discipline as attested by the fact that eight of the ten commandments are prohibitions (Exodus 20:1-19). We need the prohibitions that are set forth, not just in the Ten Commandments, but in all the life-application sections of the New Testament. Indwelling sin that remains in us has a persistent inclination toward worldly passions and needs the constant restraint of being denied its gratification.

The Christian life, however, should also be directed toward the positive expressions of Christian character, what Paul called the fruit of the Spirit in Galatians 5:22. In fact, all of Paul's ethical teaching is characterized by this twofold approach of putting off the old self and putting on the new self. For example, in Ephesians 4:22-24 he wrote, "You were taught, with regard to your former way of life, to put off your old self, which is being corrupted by its deceitful desires; to be made new in the attitude of your minds; and to put on the new self, created to be like God in true righteousness and holiness."

I like to think of this twofold approach of "putting off" and "putting on" as represented by the two blades of a pair of scissors. We readily recognize that a single scissors blade is useless as far as doing the job for which it was designed. The two blades must be joined together at the pivot point and must work in conjunction with each other to be effective. The scissors illustrates a spiritual principle: We must work simultaneously at putting off the characteristics of our old selves and putting on the characteristics of the new selves. One without the other is not effective.

Some believers seem to focus on putting off sinful practices but give little attention to what they are to put on. Too often the lives of such people become hard and brittle and probably self-righteous, since they tend to equate godliness with a defined list of "don'ts." Other believers tend to focus on putting on certain positive traits such as love, compassion, and kindness. But if they do not pay attention to the "don'ts" of Scripture, they can become careless in morality and ethics. So we need the dual focus of "putting off" and "putting on," and each should receive equal attention from us.

In the Titus passage we are considering, the positive aspect of the Christian life is expressed by the phrase, "[It teaches us] to live self-controlled, upright and godly lives in this present age." These three words—self-controlled, upright, and godly—are considered by most Bible commentators to refer to actions with regard to one's self, one's neighbor, and to God. Self-control expresses the self-restraint we need to practice toward the good and legitimate things of life, as well as the outright denial of things clearly sinful. Upright or righteous conduct refers to just and right actions toward other people, doing to them what we would have them do to us (Matthew 7:12). Godliness is having a regard for God's glory and God's will in every aspect of our lives, doing everything out of reverence and love for Him.

Matthew Henry has a very helpful description of godliness in his commentary on Titus 2:12. He wrote,

Personal and relative duties must be done in obedience to his commands, with due aim at pleasing and honouring him, from principles of holy love and fear of him. But there is an express and direct duty also that we owe to God, namely, belief and acknowledgment of his being and perfections, paying him internal and external worship and homage,—loving, fearing, and trusting in him,—depending on him, and devoting ourselves to him,—observing all those religious duties and ordinances that he has appointed,— praying to him, praising him, and meditating on his word and works.[1]

PRACTICAL CHRISTIAN LIVING
The Apostle Paul summed up our three-directional duties of the Christian life in three words: self-controlled, upright, and godly. The context of his moral description of God's saving grace, however, is a whole series of moral exhortations from Titus 2:1 through 3:2. The instructions are addressed to the practical spiritual needs of various groups—older men, older women, younger women, young men, slaves, Titus himself, and finally to all believers. From these specific instructions we can begin to "flesh out" what he means by self-controlled, upright, and godly lives.

This section of Scripture contains so many concise instructions that to elaborate on it would entail basically restating the passage. I urge you to prayerfully read it over yourself, asking God to help you evaluate your own life in light of Paul's instructions in practical Christian living. Don't just pay attention to the section that applies most to you (older men, older women, younger women, etc.). There are Christian virtues in each section that apply to all of us, regardless of age or gender.

I do call your attention to the three instances where Paul emphasized the importance of our Christian testimony before unbelievers. In Titus 2:5, he said, "so that no one will malign the word of God." In verse 8 he wrote, "so that those who oppose you may be ashamed because they have nothing bad to say about us." And then in his instructions to slaves, Paul concluded with, "so that in every way they will make the teaching about God our Savior attractive" (verse 10).

Paul was obviously concerned about the witness by life of the believers in Crete. In Romans he had said to the Jews, "God's name is blasphemed among the Gentiles because of you" (Romans 2:24), and he must have had a similar concern about the Cretan Christians. What would he say about us today? As the unbelieving world becomes increasingly hostile to true Christianity, it will be even more eager to find inconsistencies in our lives so it can ridicule God and His Word.

More than four hundred years ago the great reformer John Calvin voiced a similar concern when he wrote,

> Everything bad they [the ungodly] can seize hold of in our life is twisted maliciously against Christ and His teaching. The result is that by our fault God's sacred name is exposed to insult. The more closely we see ourselves being watched by our enemies, the more intent we should be to avoid their slanders, so that their ill-will strengthens us in the desire to do well.[2]

Therefore, as believers, we should seek to be exemplary in every aspect of our lives, doing our best for the sake of Christ and His gospel. Our work, our play, our driving, our shopping should all be done with a view that not only will unbelievers have nothing bad to say, but on the contrary, they will be attracted to the gospel that they see at work in our lives.

Another very practical presentation of everyday Christian living is found in the putting-off–putting-on section of Ephesians. I have already called attention to the statement of this basic principle in Ephesians 4:22-24. However, immediately following this statement, Paul gives specific examples of how to apply the principle. We are to put off falsehood and speak truthfully (4:25). Those who have been stealing (for example, on expense accounts or tax returns) must steal no longer. Instead they, and all of us, should learn to share with those in need (verse 28).

Paul's contrast of generosity with stealing is very instructive regarding the concept of putting on godly character as well as putting off sinful traits. If someone in our fellowship who had been stealing made a definitive break with that practice, we would rejoice over a major victory won. But Paul would not be satisfied until that person had also acquired a generous spirit of helping others in need. The person must put on generosity as well as put off dishonesty.

There are three attitudes we can have toward money and possessions:

❖"What's yours is mine; I will take it."
❖"What's mine is mine; I will keep it."
❖"What's mine is God's; I will share it."

The first attitude is that of the thief. The second is that of the typical person, including, sad to say, many Christians. The third attitude is the one each of us should seek to put on. It is not enough not to steal; we must also learn to share.

The principle of putting off–putting on is seen again in our speech (Ephesians 4:29). We are to put off unwholesome talk (not just vulgar or obscene speech, but also criticism, complaining, gossip, and the like) and put on what is constructive and builds up others. Negative emotions of bitterness, rage, and anger and sinful actions of brawling and slander are to be put off and replaced with kindness, compassion, and forgiveness (verses 31-32).

Immorality or impurity of any kind, not only in actions but also in words, thoughts, and desires, is not to be practiced—no, not even a hint of them. This leads naturally to exhortation against any form of obscenity or witty but coarse jokes. Instead, a believer's speech should be marked by thanksgiving (5:3-4).

Why does Paul set thanksgiving over against witty but coarse joking? For one thing, in the original language there is a play on words—*eucharistia* over against *eutrapolia*. But more importantly, Paul was telling us that our speech should be dominated by thanksgiving to God instead of foul speech, or even complaining speech. As he said in 1 Thessalonians 5:18, we are to "give thanks in all circumstances, for this is God's will for you in Christ Jesus."

GRACE TEACHES US

With all this emphasis on practical Christian living, however, we must not lose sight of the fact that it is grace—not law—that teaches us. When I first became a Christian I regarded the Bible largely as a rule book. My perception was that the Bible would tell me what to do (or not do), and I would simply obey. It was as easy as that, so I thought in my new Christian naiveté.

To me, then, the practical precepts of the Bible were no more than a statement of the law of God. They commanded but gave no ability to obey. Furthermore, they condemned me for my failure to obey them as I knew I ought. It seemed the more I tried, the more I failed.

I knew nothing of God's grace in enabling me to live the Christian life. I thought it was all by sheer grit and willpower. And just as importantly, I understood little of His forgiving grace through the blood of Christ. So I felt both guilty and helpless—guilty because of recurring sin patterns in my life and helpless to do anything about them.

My experience, however, was not unusual. In fact, I would say it is fairly typical, not just among new believers, but among many who have been Christians for years. That is why we need to understand that it is grace—not law—that disciplines us. Of course, Paul personified grace in the Titus passage. It is actually God in His grace, or by His grace, who disciplines us. Or to put it more plainly, God's parental training of His children is based on the principles of grace and administered in the realm of grace.

What are the principles of grace? Basically they are the two truths we studied in chapters 3 and 4. The first is the forgiveness of all our sins and the unconditional acceptance of our persons through the atoning work of Jesus Christ. The second is the deliverance from the dominion of sin and the enabling power of the Holy Spirit in us through our union with Christ.

What does it mean that God administers His discipline in the realm of grace? It means that all His teaching, training, and discipline are administered in love and for our spiritual welfare. It means that God is never angry with us, though He is often grieved at our sins. It means He does not condemn us or count our sins against us. All that He does in us and to us is done on the basis of unmerited favor. To use the words of William Hendriksen, "God's grace is his active favor bestowing the greatest gift upon those who have deserved the greatest punishment."[3]

So where the law condemns, grace forgives through the Lord Jesus Christ. Where the law commands but gives no power, grace commands but does give power through the Holy Spirit who lives and works within us.

While I was in the midst of writing this chapter, I happened to have lunch with a small group that included a professor of New Testament at one of our evangelical seminaries. He passed on to us a helpful little verse that he thought was attributable to John Bunyan, the author of *Pilgrim's Progress*, but he was unable to verify that. When he quoted the verse to us I thought, *That's what Paul meant when he said, "Grace disciplines us."*

So here it is. It's easy to memorize, and if you do so, it will help you capture the essence of what it means to be disciplined by grace:

> Run, John, run. The law commands
> But gives neither feet nor hands.
> Better news the gospel brings;
> It bids me fly and gives me wings.

How then are you being disciplined? Is it by law, or is it by grace? Of course, God *is* disciplining by His grace, but how do you perceive it? How are you seeking to respond to

His parental training? Do you accept the forgiveness of His grace, or do you labor under the burden of guilt? Are you relying on your union with Christ and the indwelling Holy Spirit for the power to respond to God's training, or is the Bible only a rule book of commands you are struggling to obey by your own willpower?

Remember, the grace that brought salvation to you is the same grace that teaches you. But you must respond on the basis of grace, not law. That is why you must "preach the gospel to yourself every day."

6

TRANSFORMED INTO HIS LIKENESS

*But we all, with unveiled face beholding as in a mirror
the glory of the Lord, are being transformed
into the same image from glory to glory,
just as from the Lord, the Spirit.*
2 CORINTHIANS 3:18, NASB

SOME THINGS IN NATURE are a complete mystery to me. How can an insect that crawls on the ground be changed into one that flies? How can a black, fuzzy, rather ugly creature be transformed into a beautiful, fascinating creature with brightly colored wings? How can a destructive insect that can literally strip a tree of its leaves (at least a swarm of them can) become a dainty creature that can land on the petal of a flower blossom without defacing it? In short, how can a caterpillar become a butterfly?

I don't understand the process, but I know the word for it. It is *metamorphosis*. That five-syllable, "eight-cylinder" word is used to describe what happens when a caterpillar spins a hard cocoon around itself and some days later emerges as a butterfly.

A lot of things in the spiritual realm are also a complete mystery to me. How can a person who is indifferent or hostile toward God become a deeply committed follower of Jesus Christ? How can a person who is a slave to destructive sinful habits become a person who is self-controlled, gentle, and compassionate? How can a fanatical, self-righteous Jew named Saul of Tarsus become the humble, self-effacing Paul, the apostle to the Gentiles?

Again, I don't understand the process, but I know the name for it. In 2 Corinthians 3:18, Paul calls it transformation (being transformed). The Greek word for transformation is *metamorphoomai*. You can readily see that our English word *metamorphosis* is essentially a transliteration of *metamorphoomai*. I find it somewhat fascinating and instructive that Paul uses the same word that describes the transformation of a caterpillar into a butterfly to describe the spiritual transformation in the life of a Christian. The process is just as mysterious, and the results are even more striking.

Actually the process of transformation that Paul describes very briefly in 2 Corinthians 3:18 is called *sanctification*. Here is another one of those "eight-cylinder" words, as I call them. It is a word that is not part of our daily vocabulary, and perhaps even sounds a bit pretentious. But it is an important scriptural word that we ought to become familiar with if we desire to pursue holiness. Sanctification is the work of the Holy Spirit in us whereby our inner being is progressively changed, freeing us more and more from sinful traits and developing within us over time the virtues of Christlike character. However, though sanctification is the work of the Holy Spirit in us, it does involve our whole-hearted response in obedience and the regular use of the spiritual disciplines that are instruments of sanctification.

REGENERATION

Sanctification actually begins at the time of our conversion, when by an act called regeneration, or the new birth, the principle of spiritual life is planted within us. This work of regeneration is promised in such Old Testament prophecies as Jeremiah 31:33, where God says, "I will put my law in their minds and write it on their hearts." And in Ezekiel 36:26-27 He says, "I will give you a new heart and put a new spirit in you; I will remove from you your heart of stone and give you a heart of flesh. And I will put my Spirit in you and move you to follow my decrees and be careful to keep my laws."

In the New Testament, Paul also described regeneration in 2 Corinthians 5:17—"Therefore, if anyone is in Christ, he is a new creation; the old has gone, the new has come!" And again in Titus 3:5—"He saved us through the washing of rebirth [or regeneration, as it is translated in many versions of the Bible] and renewal by the Holy Spirit."

Note the radical change that is explicitly described in each of these Scripture passages. God will put His law in our minds and write it on our hearts. That is, He will give us a new disposition that, instead of being hostile to God's law, actually delights in it. The law, which before was merely external, is now written in our hearts by the Spirit of God so that we are moved to obedience.

The heart of stone is transformed into a heart of flesh. "Heart of stone" is a figurative expression for a hard heart, one that is insensible to the things of God and unable to receive any impressions of divine truth. The heart of flesh represents a soft and tender heart, one that is able and willing to receive and act upon the truths of God's Word. Matthew Henry says of this verse, "Renewing grace works as great a change in the soul as the turning of a dead stone into living flesh."[1]

Paul said in 2 Corinthians 5:17 that when a person is united to Christ, there is a new creation. A Christian is a radically changed person the moment he or she trusts Christ. This doesn't mean we become "saints" in practice overnight. It does mean a new creation—a new principle of life—has been planted within us by the Holy Spirit, and we can never be the same again.

The expression "born again," from John 3:3-8, is usually taken to mean no more than being saved from the penalty of sin. According to Jesus, it means to be born of the Spirit (John 3:6,8), that is, to be given new life. Paul said the same thing in Titus 3:5 when he spoke of renewal by the Holy Spirit.

This act of regeneration or new birth by which a person enters the Kingdom of God (John 3:5), is solely the work of God the Holy Spirit. Thus it is entirely a work of grace, just as justification is. It is also an instantaneous act of God. The moment we are justified we are also regenerated. A person cannot be justified without being regenerated.

Again I am concerned that there are thousands of professing Christians who think they have been justified, who think their sins are forgiven and that they are on their way to Heaven, who show no evidence of the regenerating work of the Holy Spirit in their lives. I fear for them that they will one day hear those awful words from the lips of Christ, "I never knew you. Away from me, you evildoers!" (Matthew 7:23).

Lest I be misunderstood at this point, let me say emphatically that the solution for these people is not to change their conduct so that they might see some evidences of regeneration. The solution is to come to Jesus, renouncing any confidence in their own goodness, confessing themselves to be sinners in the sight of God, and trusting entirely in His atoning work. They will then be truly justified (saved from the penalty of sin) and will at the same time be genuinely regenerated (made new creations in Christ). The evidence of regeneration will then be apparent to them and to others around them.

SANCTIFICATION

Regeneration, then, is the beginning of sanctification, or to use Paul's word in 2 Corinthians 3:18, of transformation. Sanctification, then, is the carrying out of regeneration to its intended end. William Plumer, a nineteenth-century Presbyterian minister, wrote, "Regeneration is an *act* of God's Spirit. Sanctification is a *work* of God's Spirit, consequent upon that act. . . . In regeneration we become 'newborn babes;' in sanctification we attain the stature of full-grown men in Christ Jesus."[2]

The question is sometimes asked, "What is the relationship of sanctification to justification? Can a person be justified but not sanctified?" The answer is, justification and sanctification are inseparable. God never gives justification without sanctification (see 1 Corinthians 1:30 and 6:11). Both have their source in the infinite love and free grace of God. Both are accomplished by faith. In justification we rely on what Christ did *for* us on the cross. In sanctification we rely on Christ to work *in* us by His Holy Spirit. In justification, as well as regeneration, God acts alone. In sanctification He works in us but elicits our response to cooperate with Him.

Quoting William Plumer again,

> Justification is an act of God complete at once and for ever. Sanctification is a work of God begun in regeneration, conducted through life and completed at death. The former is equal and perfect in all; the latter is not equal in all, nor perfect in any till they lay aside the flesh. In justification God imputes [that is, credits] to us the righteousness of Christ; in sanctification he [imparts] grace, and enables us to exercise it.[3]

The Holy Spirit's work is a work of grace in two respects. In an earlier book, *Transforming Grace*, I showed that the Scriptures use the word *grace* in two distinct but related ways. The broader, more common meaning is God's unmerited favor to us through Jesus Christ. But there are several instances in Scripture where the meaning is God's divine assistance to us through the Holy Spirit.[4] But even this divine assistance is a result of God's unmerited favor. So whether we think of sanctification as an undeserved blessing, which it is, or as the gracious work of the Holy Spirit in us, it is indeed a work of grace.

Our part, that is, our response to the Holy Spirit's work and our cooperation with Him in His work is the pursuit of holiness. We will be considering our part in sanctification beginning in chapter 7. But for now, I want to emphasize that the pursuit of holiness, though requiring diligent effort on our part, is dependent upon the enabling power of the

Holy Spirit. The Apostle Paul expressed this principle of dependent discipline quite succinctly in Philippians 4:13: "I can do everything through him who gives me strength." Paul did the work, in that case, learning to be content. But he did it through the enabling strength of the Holy Spirit. It is difficult to grasp this principle of being responsible yet dependent. But it is absolutely vital that we grasp it and live by it.

THE GOAL

The goal of sanctification is likeness to our Lord Jesus Christ. Paul said in 2 Corinthians 3:18 that we "are being transformed into his likeness." In Romans 8:29 he said that God "predestined [all believers] to be conformed to the likeness of his Son." Christlikeness is God's goal for all who trust in Christ, and that should be our goal also.

Both words, *transformed* and *conformed*, have a common root, *form*, meaning a pattern or a mold. "Being transformed" refers to the process; conformed refers to the finished product. Jesus is our pattern or mold. We are being transformed so that we will eventually be conformed to the likeness of Jesus.

Sanctification or holiness (the words are somewhat interchangeable), then, is conformity to the likeness of Jesus Christ. We see this same idea expressed in different wording in other New Testament scriptures. In Ephesians 4:24, Paul said our new self is *"created to be like God* in true righteousness and holiness." The writer of Hebrews stated that God disciplines us, "that we may *share in his holiness"* (Hebrews 12:10), and in 1 Peter 1:16, the Apostle Peter quotes an Old Testament passage where God said, "Be holy, because *I am holy"* (emphasis added in each scripture quoted).

How can we know whether we are being transformed more and more into the likeness of Christ? We begin by studying His character. One of my favorite descriptions of Christ is that He "loved righteousness and hated wickedness" (Hebrews 1:9). Jesus did not just *act* righteously, He *loved* righteousness. In His humanity He loved equity, fairness, justice, and upright dealings with others. At the same time He *hated* wickedness. Jesus hated sin as sin. We often hate the consequences of sin (even if it seems to be no more than the guilt feelings that follow sin), but I suspect we seldom hate sin as sin. We saw in chapter 2 that sin is a rebellion against God's authority, a despising of His person, and a defiance of His commands. Do we truly hate sin when we see it in our own lives because of the despicable nature of it? To the extent we do, we are being transformed into His likeness.

Another Scripture that is helpful to me is John 6:38— "For I have come down from heaven not to do my will but to do the will of him who sent me." Jesus' entire goal in His earthly life was to do the will of His Father, even though that will culminated in Jesus laying down His life for His sheep. If we are going to become more and more like Him, we must grow toward that same goal of seeking His will. To be like Jesus is not just to stop committing a few obvious sins such as lying, cheating, gossiping, and thinking impure thoughts. To be like Jesus is to always seek to do the will of the Father. That is a very high standard. We frequently desire to do our own will, resulting in actions that may not appear to be sinful in themselves. But they are sinful if they are not the Father's will.

Not only did Jesus do the will of the Father, not only was that His whole goal in life, but Psalm 40:8 tells us that He *delighted* to do the will of the Father.[5] To become like Jesus, then, is to come to the place where we delight to do the will of God, however sacrificial or unpleasant that will may seem to us at the time, simply because it is *His* will.

Then there is Jesus' statement in John 8:29, "for I always do what pleases him [the Father]." Everything Jesus did was done with the aim of pleasing the Father. And of course, He perfectly realized that aim. What about us? How often do we think, speak, or act with the aim of pleasing the Father? Of course, we will never attain that aim to the extent Jesus did, but the question remains, what is our aim? Is it to please the Father in all we do, or is it to just get through life as comfortably as we can?

Consider also that God looks at our motives as well as our actions (see 1 Chronicles 28:9, Proverbs 16:2, 1 Corinthians 4:5). We may do or say the right thing outwardly, but what is our motive? Is it to please the Father, or is it sometimes to feel good about ourselves, or to look good to others? I'm not saying that we should always be questioning our motives, I'm just attempting to paint a picture to some degree of what it means to be transformed more and more into the likeness of Christ.

A PROCESS

We can easily see from the pattern of Jesus' life that conformity to Him is a lifelong process, and a goal that will never be attained completely in this life. That is why Paul refers to the continual change being wrought in us with his expression in 2 Corinthians 3:18, "with ever-increasing glory," or as it is more literally translated in the *New American Standard Bible*, "from glory to glory." That is, as the Spirit of God works in us, we progress from one stage of glory to the next. As Charles Hodge wrote, "The transformation is carried forward without intermission, from the first scarce discernible resemblance, to full conformity to the image of Christ, both as to soul and body."[6]

Because sanctification is a process, there will always be conflict within us between the "flesh," or the sinful nature, and the Holy Spirit. This conflict is described by Paul in Galatians 5:17—"For the sinful nature desires what is contrary to the Spirit, and the Spirit what is contrary to the sinful nature. They are in conflict with each other, so that you do not do what you want." He elaborated on this struggle in greater detail in Romans 7:14-25, where he said such things as, "I know that nothing good lives in me, that is, in my sinful nature. For I have the desire to do what is good, but I cannot carry it out" (verse 18).

I realize that not all Bible expositors regard the tension described in Romans 7:14-25 as descriptive of a normal Christian experience, let alone of someone who is vigorously pursuing holiness. Yet what honest Christian would not admit to the frequent gap between his or her spiritual desires and actual performance? Which of us would not concede that "When I want to do good, evil is right there with me" (verse 21) is a frequent lament?

The comments of John Murray are most helpful at this point. He wrote,

> The presence of sin in the believer involves conflict in his heart and life. If there is remaining, indwelling sin, there must be the conflict which Paul describes in Romans 7:14ff. It is futile to argue that this conflict is not normal. If there is still sin to any degree in one who is indwelt by the Holy Spirit, then there is tension, yes, contradiction, within the heart of that person. Indeed, the more sanctified the person is, the more conformed he is to the image of his Saviour, the more he must recoil against every lack of conformity to the holiness of God. The deeper his apprehension of the majesty of God, the greater the intensity of his love to God, the more persistent his yearning for the attainment of the prize of the high calling of God in Christ Jesus, the more conscious will he be of the gravity of the sin which remains and the more poignant will be his detestation of it.[7]

Think of yourself walking into a room where the lighting is controlled by a dimmer switch. As you walk in, the lighting is dim and you see the furniture all in place, no newspapers lying around, and no dirty cups on the coffee table. The room looks neat and clean. But as you turn up the wattage in the lights, you begin to see dust on the furniture, smudges on the walls, chips in the paint, and threadbare spots in the carpet. The room that looked all right in the dim light suddenly appears dirty and unattractive under the full glare of the brighter light.

That is what happens in the life of a person who is pursuing holiness. At first your life may appear fairly good because you've been a decent sort of person and no gross sins are visible. Then the Holy Spirit begins to "turn up the wattage" of His Word and reveal the more subtle, "refined" sins of which you were not even aware. Or perhaps you were aware of certain thoughts or actions but had not realized they were sinful.

An even better analogy might be the shining of a spotlight into the shadowy recesses of an old house. The Holy Spirit is continually shining His spotlight of conviction into the recesses of our hearts, revealing sinful attitudes and actions of which we were not aware. These newly discovered sins are usually dismaying and discomforting to us. And the more holy a person is, the more he or she is dismayed. Then as we attempt to deal with these sins, we discover that they are stubbornly entrenched in our habits of life and are not easily dislodged. Or a sinful habit we thought had been decisively dealt with reasserts itself, and we seem powerless before its onslaught. All these experiences set up the tension within us that Paul described in the latter half of Romans 7.

Does this mean then that we are no better off than the unbeliever who struggles with some habit he or she wants to be rid of? By no means. John Murray offers helpful insight into the difference between the struggle of a believer with sin and that of an unbeliever with some undesirable habits. He wrote,

> There must be a constant and increasing appreciation that though sin still remains it does not have the mastery. There is a total difference between surviving sin and reigning sin, the regenerate in conflict with sin and the unregenerate complacent to sin. It is one thing for sin to live in us: it is another for us to live in sin.[8]

The Puritan Samuel Bolton also helps us see the distinction between the believer's struggle with sin and the dominion of sin in the unbeliever. He wrote,

> We [believers] still have the presence of sin, nay, the stirrings and workings of corruption. These make us to have many a sad heart and wet eye. Yet Christ has thus far freed us from sin; it shall not have dominion. There may be the turbulence, but not the prevalence of sin. . . . [Sin] may get into the throne of the heart and play the tyrant in this or that particular act of sin, but it shall never more be as a king there.[9]

Sin is like a defeated army in a civil war that, instead of surrendering and laying down its arms, simply fades into the countryside, from which it continues to wage a guerrilla war of harassment and sabotage against the government forces. Sin as a reigning power is defeated in the life of the believer, but it will *never* surrender. It will continue to harass us and seek to sabotage our Christian lives as long as we live.

It is important for us to understand this difference between the unbeliever living complacently in sin and the believer struggling against sin. If we are going to pursue holiness, we must accept the fact that there will be continual tension within us between our desires and our performance. As British theologian J. I. Packer so often says, our reach will always exceed our grasp.

THE AGENT

Who is responsible for this transformation? The Holy Spirit is. Paul said in 2 Corinthians 3:18 that we are being transformed by "the Lord, who is the Spirit." The verb *being transformed* is passive, that is, something is being done *to* us, not *by* us. This does not mean we have no responsibility in sanctification. It means that in the final analysis it is the

Spirit of God who transforms us. He calls on us to cooperate and to do the part He assigns us to do, but He is the one who works deep within our character to change us.

The pursuit of holiness has been a major object of my thoughts and study for almost thirty-five years. Over that time, I have come to realize—both from personal study and observation of my life—that the deep work of spiritual transformation of my soul has been what the Holy Spirit has done, not what I have done. I can to some degree change my conduct, but only He can change my heart.

Several passages of Scripture emphasize the fact that sanctification is primarily the work of the Holy Spirit. In 1 Thessalonians 5:23-24 Paul said, "May God himself, the God of peace, sanctify you through and through. May your whole spirit, soul and body be kept blameless at the coming of our Lord Jesus Christ. The one who calls you is faithful and he will do it." Note that it is God Himself who will sanctify us "through and through." In other words, He will bring the process to completion.

Again Paul wrote in Philippians 1:6, "being confident of this, that he who began a good work in you will carry it on to completion until the day of Christ Jesus." Finally the writer of Hebrews prayed that God will "work in us what is pleasing to him" (Hebrews 13:21). Although these passages speak of God in a nonspecific sense, or use the pronoun *He*, we know from other scriptures that the work of sanctification within the Trinity is primarily the work of the Holy Spirit (2 Thessalonians 2:13, 1 Peter 1:2). This being true, we ought to pray daily for His work of sanctification within us. One of my favorite prayers is to take the words of Hebrews 13:21 and ask that He will work in me what is pleasing to Him. (We'll look more at the place of prayer in sanctification in chapter 8.)

The Spirit of God has indeed given us certain responsibilities in the sanctifying process. In fact, the Bible is filled with exhortations, challenges, and commands to obey, as well as spiritual disciplines to be practiced. We will consider

these beginning in chapter 7. However, I am now emphasizing the Spirit's work because we tend to lose sight of the
fact that He is the agent of sanctification.

The way the Spirit operates in our lives to sanctify us is
shrouded in mystery. Paul said He works in us "to will and to
act according to his good purpose" (Philippians 2:13), but he
never tells us just how the Holy Spirit interacts with, or works
on, our human spirit. I like to know how things work, and I
used to try to figure out how the Holy Spirit interacts with
our spirit, but I finally realized it was a futile pursuit. On this
subject the comments of John Murray are again helpful: "We
do not know the mode of the Spirit's indwelling nor the
mode of his efficient working in the hearts and minds and
wills of God's people by which they are progressively
cleansed from the defilement of sin and more and more trans-
figured after the image of Christ."[10]

We will often be conscious of the Holy Spirit's working
in our lives and will even be able to discern what He is
doing to some extent, especially in those instances where He
elicits a conscious response from us. But, to again use the
words of John Murray, "we must not suppose that the measure of our understanding or experience is the measure of
the Spirit's working."[11]

THE MEANS
Although the Holy Spirit is the agent of sanctification and
Himself works in us in this mysterious fashion, it is also true
that He uses rational and understandable means to sanctify
us. Some of these means, such as adversities and the exhortation and encouragement of others, are outside of our control to initiate. With other means, such as the learning and
application of Scripture and the frequent use of prayer, He
expects us to take the initiative. We will come to these in
later chapters. For now I want to focus on the one specific
means that Paul mentions in 2 Corinthians 3:18, that is,
beholding the glory of Christ.

Paul wrote, "But we all, with unveiled face beholding as

in a mirror the glory of the Lord, are being transformed" (NASB).[12] That is, beholding the glory of the Lord is one means the Spirit uses to transform us.

What is the glory of the Lord that Paul referred to, and how does beholding it transform us? First, the glory of the Lord denotes the presence of God and all that He is in all of His attributes—His infiniteness, eternalness, holiness, sovereignty, goodness, etc. In other words, God is glorious in all of His being and all of His works. However, in the context of 2 Corinthians 3:18, Paul was contrasting the glory of the law given by Moses with the far-surpassing glory of the gospel (see 2 Corinthians 3:7-11). Then in 2 Corinthians 4:4, he spoke of "the gospel of the glory of Christ." This means the glory of Christ is good news, for the word *gospel* means good news.

This close connection between the gospel and Christ's glory leads me to believe that Paul was in this instance thinking of the glory of Christ, especially as it is revealed in the gospel. The law reveals the glory of God in His righteousness; the gospel reveals the glory of God in *both* His righteousness and grace. Christ's death reveals the righteousness of God in that it satisfied the justice of God, but it also reveals the grace of God in that it was the means of salvation to those who deserve only eternal wrath.

Furthermore, the gospel reveals the wisdom of God in devising such an infinitely magnificent way of meeting our desperate need without sacrificing His holiness and justice. And it reveals the power of God, both in His raising Jesus from the dead and in raising us from spiritual death to a new life in Christ. So the gospel pulls together and harmonizes all these glorious attributes of the Lord: His righteousness with His grace, His justice with His mercy, His power with His love, His wisdom with His patience and compassion.

It seems, though, that God desires to magnify His grace in a special way to us, for Paul wrote in Ephesians 2:6-7, "And God raised us up with Christ and seated us with him in the heavenly realms in Christ Jesus, in order that in the coming ages he might show the incomparable riches of his grace, expressed in his kindness to us in Christ Jesus." The key phrase is that God might show the incomparable riches of his grace. This is God's goal in salvation of fallen human beings: the exaltation of His grace shown to us in Christ.

James Fraser (1700–1769), an obscure Scottish pastor, wrote a masterful treatise on sanctification that was recognized as a classic in its day and has recently been reprinted. In this book he has this to say about the glory of the gospel:

> It is the gospel that exhibits God's highest glory, which he chiefly designs to display before sinful men, even that glory of God that shineth in the face of Christ. It is the gospel that sets forth the glory of Christ, and by which the Holy Spirit himself is glorified; and it is it that will be honoured with the concomitant [accompanying] influence of the Holy Spirit. . . .
>
> If it should now be asked what is that special doctrine of the gospel, and, strictly speaking, the doctrine of faith? I shall answer briefly—
>
> All revealed truth ought to be greatly valued, and received by faith; and, if properly used, may be subservient to the main subject and design of the gospel. But the special subject of the gospel is Christ; and preaching Christ, according to the light and direction of the word of God, is preaching the gospel. . . . To preach Christ the SAVIOR and the LORD, is the sum of gospel-preaching.[13]

This then is the glory that has a transforming effect on us. It is the glory of Christ revealed in the gospel, the good news that Jesus died in our place as our representative to free us not only from the penalty of sin but also from its dominion. A clear understanding and appropriation of the gospel, which gives freedom from sin's guilt and sin's grip, is, in the hands of the Holy Spirit, a chief means of sanctification.

To the degree that we feel we are on a legal or performance relationship with God, to that degree our progress in sanctification is impeded. A legal mode of thinking gives indwelling sin an advantage, because nothing cuts the nerve of the desire to pursue holiness as much as a sense of guilt. On the contrary, nothing so motivates us to deal with sin in our lives as does the understanding and application of the two truths that our sins are forgiven and the dominion of sin is broken because of our union with Christ.

Robert Haldane, in his commentary on Romans, quotes from a previous writer identified only as "Mr. Romaine," who said, "No sin can be crucified either in heart or life, unless it be first pardoned in conscience; because there will be want of faith to receive the strength of Jesus, by whom alone it can be crucified. If it be not mortified [put to death] in its guilt, it cannot be subdued in its power."[14]

We will be studying the discipline of putting sin to death, or subduing it, in chapter 11. For now, however, we should consider the connection Mr. Romaine drew between sin's being pardoned in our consciences and our ability to rely upon Christ for the strength to subdue it. The cleansing of our consciences from the *guilt* of sin must precede our efforts to deal with the *presence* of sin in our daily lives.

In the words of Hebrews 9:14, it is "the blood of Christ" that will "cleanse our consciences from acts that lead to death [that is, from sinful acts], so that we may serve the living God!" We cannot serve God or pursue holiness with any vigor at all if we are dealing with a guilty conscience. Therefore we need the gospel to remind us that our sins are forgiven in Christ, and that "the blood of Jesus Christ, his Son, purifies us from all sin" (1 John 1:7).

Our specific responsibility in the pursuit of holiness as seen in 2 Corinthians 3:18, then, is to behold the glory of the Lord as it is displayed in the gospel. The gospel is the "mirror" through which we now behold His beauty. One day we shall see Christ, not as in a mirror, but face to face. Then, "we shall be like him, for we shall see him as he is" (1 John 3:2). Until then we behold Him in the gospel. Therefore, we must "preach the gospel to ourselves every day."

To behold the glory of Christ in the gospel is a discipline. It is a habit we must develop by practice as we learn to preach the gospel to ourselves. As I have repeatedly said, although sanctification is the work of the Holy Spirit, it is a work in which He involves us. In later chapters we will be looking at other disciplines that we must practice in the pursuit of holiness. But none is more important than the discipline of beholding the glory of Christ in the "mirror" of the gospel.

7

OBEYING THE GREAT COMMANDMENT

"Teacher, which is the greatest commandment in the Law?"
Jesus replied: "'Love the Lord your God with all your
heart and with all your soul and with all your mind.' This
is the first and greatest commandment. And the second is
like it: 'Love your neighbor as yourself.' All the Law and the
Prophets hang on these two commandments."
MATTHEW 22:36-40

I ENJOY FELLOWSHIP with God, and often in the morning I awaken with the words in my mind, "I love You, Lord."

For a time, however, it seemed as if I could hear the still, small voice of God in my mind saying, "Oh, really?" After a few of those occasions I began to reflect on what I was saying. What did I mean when I said, "I love You, Lord"? And why did I get the impression that perhaps God was not all that impressed with my sincere expressions of love to Him?

When I said, "I love You, Lord," I was expressing a sense of delight in God and an eager anticipation of fellowship with Him during my early-morning quiet time. I could hardly wait to get dressed. I wanted to be with God; to enjoy His Word; to share my heart with Him in prayer; and in the words of David,

> to gaze upon the beauty of the LORD
> and to seek him in his temple. (Psalm 27:4)

What is wrong with that? Are not those noble, godly desires? Why was I frequently getting this nagging thought in my mind that perhaps God was not all that convinced of my love?

I began to reflect on the question, What does it mean to love God? This is an important question. After all, Jesus said that the *greatest* commandment is to "Love the Lord your God with all your heart and with all your soul and with all your mind" (Matthew 22:37). To love God with all my heart and soul and mind obviously means to love Him with all my being, with everything I have. And if I am to love God with this total wholeheartedness, then I need to know what it means to love God. So I began to study this passage in Matthew.

The first thing I saw from Jesus' reply in Matthew 22 is that He actually quoted from the Old Testament. The question that had been put to Him was, "Which is the greatest commandment in the Law?" So Jesus went right back to the Law, specifically to Deuteronomy 6:5, and quoted that scripture as His answer. I decided, then, to study this greatest commandment as it was originally given in the Old Testament.

To help us understand what God is saying to us, we need to see Deuteronomy 6:5 in its context. For your convenience I am going to reproduce Deuteronomy 6:1-8 so that you can more easily follow me in the primary lesson I learned from this Scripture.

> These are the commands, decrees and laws the LORD your God directed me to teach you to observe in the land that you are crossing the Jordan to possess, so that you, your children and their children after them may fear the LORD your God as long as you live by keeping all his decrees and commands that I give you, and so that you may enjoy long life. Hear, O Israel, and be careful to obey so that it may go well with you and that you may increase greatly in a land flowing with milk and honey, just as the LORD, the God of

your fathers, promised you. Hear, O Israel: The LORD
our God, the LORD is one. Love the LORD your God
with all your heart and with all your soul and with all
your strength. These commandments that I give you
today are to be upon your hearts. Impress them on
your children. Talk about them when you sit at home
and when you walk along the road, when you lie
down and when you get up. Tie them as symbols on
your hands and bind them on your foreheads.

HOW TO LOVE GOD

As you read these verses from Deuteronomy, one thing that
becomes clear is that the primary message is obedience to
God. Notice how words such as *commands*, *decrees*, and *laws*
are prominent (see verses 1,2,6). Then note how obedience
to these commands, decrees, and laws is emphasized.

We are to *observe* them (verse 1), *keep* them (verse 2), and
be careful to *obey* them (verse 3). They are to be upon our
hearts (verse 6). We are to impress them on our children and
talk about them continually; that is, when we sit at home,
walk along the road, lie down, and get up (verse 7). We are
to use all manner of reminder devices to keep His commands continually before us.

For the Israelites that meant tying them on their hands
and foreheads (verse 8) and writing them on their door-
frames and gates (verse 9). For us, it might mean a "Post-It"
note with a pertinent verse of Scripture stuck on the bath-
room mirror or the clock on our desk. For a friend of mine it
means a three-by-five card with a scripture for the day written on it that he carries in his shirt pocket and refers to
throughout the day. For another friend of mine who had a
problem with a "heavy foot" on the accelerator pedal, it
meant taping a card onto his dashboard on which he had
paraphrased 1 John 2:6—"Whoever claims to live in Him
must drive as Jesus would drive." Of course, the most obvious reminder device is the discipline of Scripture memorization. Daily review and meditation on key passages is far

and away the most effective means of keeping God's commands continually before us.

It is in the midst of this strong emphasis to the Jews on obedience to God's Law, and on the practical necessity of keeping its precepts always before them so they would obey, that we find the greatest commandment, "Love the LORD your God with all your heart and with all your soul and with all your strength" (verse 5). Therefore I concluded that, whatever else might be involved in loving God with all my heart, obedience to His law was certainly a major part of it.

(Again I want to remind you that when I speak of the law of God as it applies to us today, I am referring to the permanent moral law of God that is binding upon every human being. I am not referring to the law given to Israel through Moses, some of which was temporary, such as the ceremonial law and the civil law.)

This equating of obedience to God with love to God is a prominent feature of the book of Deuteronomy. Without trying to be exhaustive, I found six other passages in the book where love and obedience are tied together. To help us feel the impact of this strong repetitive emphasis they are quoted below:

> And now, O Israel, what does the LORD your God ask of you but to fear the LORD your God, to walk in all his ways, to love him, to serve the LORD your God with all your heart and with all your soul, and to observe the LORD's commands and decrees that I am giving you today for your own good? (10:12-13)

> So if you faithfully obey the commands I am giving you today—to love the LORD your God and to serve him with all your heart and with all your soul. (11:13)

> If you carefully observe all these commands I am giving you to follow—to love the LORD your God, to walk in all his ways and to hold fast to him. (11:22)

Because you carefully follow all these laws I command you today—to love the LORD your God and to walk always in his ways. (19:9)

The LORD your God will circumcise your hearts and the hearts of your descendants, so that you may love him with all your heart and with all your soul, and live. . . . You will again obey the LORD and follow all his commands I am giving you today. (30:6,8)

This day I call heaven and earth as witnesses against you that I have set before you life and death, blessings and curses. Now choose life, so that you and your children may live and that you may love the LORD your God, listen to his voice, and hold fast to him. For the LORD is your life, and he will give you many years in the land he swore to give to your fathers, Abraham, Isaac and Jacob. (30:19-20)

It should not surprise us that obedience to God's law is a major part of loving Him. After all, Jesus said, "Whoever has my commands and obeys them, he is the one who loves me. He who loves me will be loved by my Father, and I too will love him and show myself to him" (John 14:21; see also verses 15, 23). And the Apostle John wrote, "This is love for God: to obey his commands" (1 John 5:3). I have known John 14:21 for years. I have preached it and written about it. I have taught that the proof of our love to God is our obedience to Him. Or to put it another way, our love to God will always manifest itself in obedience to Him.

CRUISE-CONTROL OBEDIENCE
So what is new? What did I learn from my study of Matthew 22:37 and Deuteronomy 6:5 that I didn't know before? What I saw was the intensity and wholeheartedness with which I should obey God. If we are to love God with all our heart

and soul and mind, and if obedience is a major part of such love, then it follows that we are to obey Him with all our heart, soul, and mind. We are to put everything we have into obedience to Him.

My observation is that most of us who are believers practice what I call a "cruise-control" approach to obedience. Many cars today have a convenient feature called cruise control. When you are driving on the highway you can accelerate to your desired speed, push the cruise-control button, and take your foot from the accelerator pedal. Some mechanism attached to the engine will then maintain your desired speed, and you can ease back and relax a little. You don't have to watch your speedometer to make sure you're not going to get a ticket for speeding, and you no longer have to experience the fatigue that comes with constant foot pressure on the accelerator. It's very convenient and relatively relaxing. It's a great feature on cars.

However, we tend to obey God in the same way. To continue the driving analogy, we press the accelerator pedal of obedience until we have brought our behavior up to a certain level or "speed." The level of obedience is most often determined by the behavior standard of other Christians around us. We don't want to lag behind them because we want to be as spiritual as they are. At the same time, we're not eager to forge ahead of them because we wouldn't want to be different. We want to just comfortably blend in with the level of obedience of those around us.

Once we have arrived at this comfortable level of obedience, we push the "cruise-control" button in our hearts, ease back, and relax. Our particular Christian culture then takes over and keeps us going at the accepted level of conduct. We don't have to watch the speed-limit signs in God's Word, and we certainly don't have to experience the fatigue that comes with seeking to obey Him with all our heart, soul, and mind. This then is what I call "cruise-control" obedience, and I fear it is descriptive of many of us much, if not all, of the time.

RACE-CAR OBEDIENCE

By contrast consider race-car drivers. They wouldn't think of using a cruise control. They are not interested in blending in with the speed of those around them. They are not out for a Sunday afternoon drive. They want to win the race.

Race-car drivers are totally focused on their driving. Their foot is always on the accelerator as they try to push their car to the outer limits of its mechanical ability and endurance. Their eye is always on the track as they press to its limit their own skill in negotiating the turns on the track and the hazards of other cars around them. They are driving with all their heart, soul, and mind.

This is what it means to love God with all our heart and soul and mind. It means to obey Him with all our heart and soul and mind. It means, in the words of Hebrews 12:14, to "make every effort . . . to be holy," and in the words of the Apostle Peter, to "make every effort" to add to our faith the various facets of Christian character (2 Peter 1:5-7).

The Apostle Paul didn't have auto races and cruise controls to use as illustrations, so he used the metaphor of a footrace. Here is how he put it in 1 Corinthians 9:24-27—

> Do you not know that in a race all the runners run, but only one gets the prize? Run in such a way as to get the prize. Everyone who competes in the games goes into strict training. They do it to get a crown that will not last; but we do it to get a crown that will last forever. Therefore I do not run like a man running aimlessly; I do not fight like a man beating the air. No, I beat my body and make it my slave so that after I have preached to others, I myself will not be disqualified for the prize.

Do you see the similarity to our contemporary illustration? The footracer running aimlessly or the boxer beating the air is the same person out for a Sunday drive with his or her cruise control on. The runner striving for the prize who goes into strict training and beats his or her body—that is, subdues its desires—is like the race-car driver who drives with all his or her heart and soul and mind. And Moses and Jesus and Paul all said this is the way we should live the Christian life.

God is not impressed with our worship on Sunday morning at church if we are practicing "cruise-control" obedience the rest of the week. You may sing with reverent zest or great emotional fervor, but your worship is only as pleasing to God as the obedience that accompanies it.

This is why the Holy Spirit was creating this sense of uneasiness in my mind over my professed love for God. I wasn't living with some flagrant sin in my life, I was simply living in a "cruise-control" mode of obedience. I had lost the commitment and intensity that is implied in the "pursuit" of holiness. I wasn't seeking to obey God's law with all my heart and soul and mind. Instead I had settled into a comfortable routine, in which there were no major vices, but neither was there an all-out effort to obey God in every area of life, especially in interpersonal relationships.

We *should* delight in God. We should eagerly anticipate fellowship with Him during the quiet time and even throughout the entire day. It is healthy to want to gaze upon His beauty and to seek Him in His temple. The Westminster Shorter Catechism answers the question "What is the chief end of man?" by saying, "Man's chief end is to glorify God and to enjoy Him forever." We are not only to glorify God, we are to enjoy Him forever, both in this life and in eternity.

So the enjoyment of God and the desire to fellowship with Him and to worship Him are certainly important dimensions of our love to God. But the most important dimension is our wholehearted obedience: our desire to obey Him with all our heart, soul, and mind.

AN ACCEPTABLE MOTIVE
Although obedience is the primary way we express our love to God, it is not the same as love. Love is essentially a

motive. Someone has made the point that love is a verb. For example, I am to love my wife as Christ loved the Church (Ephesians 5:25). Jesus said we are to love our enemies (Matthew 5:44). In each instance love is used as a verb. So then, it is correct that love is a verb, not a feeling. I am to love my enemies without regard to my feelings toward them.

In another sense, however, love is not a verb but the motive that prompts and guides other verbs; that is, certain actions. For example, I love my enemies, first by forgiving them for their harmful actions toward me, and then by seeking their welfare in appropriate ways. The verbs in this sentence are *forgive* and *seek.* Love always needs other verbs to give it hands and feet. By itself it can do nothing. This can be seen in 1 Corinthians 13 where Paul uses love as a noun, the subject of a whole list of action statements. Love is patient, love is kind, it does not envy, it does not boast, etc.

The converse truth, though, is that love gives validity to my actions and makes them acceptable to God. I can seek the welfare of my enemies so they hopefully will be nice to me or not harm me again. That is not love; it is manipulation. It is looking out for my welfare under the guise of looking out for theirs.

Love for God, then, is the only acceptable motive for obedience to Him. This love may express itself in a reverence for Him and a desire to please Him, but those expressions must spring from love. Without the motive of love, my apparent obedience may be essentially self-serving. Negatively, I may fear God will punish me, or at least withhold His blessing from me, because of some disobedience. I may abstain from a particular sinful action out of fear I will be found out or because I don't want to feel guilty afterward.

Positively, I may be seeking to earn God's blessing through some pious actions. I may conform to a certain standard of conduct because I want to fit in with and be accepted by the Christian culture in which I live. I might even obey outwardly because I have a compliant temperament, and it is simply my "nature" to obey my parents, or my teacher, or civil authorities, or even God.

All of these motives—both negative and positive—may result in an outward form of obedience, but it is not obedience from the heart. Our behavior may appear outstanding to other people but not be acceptable to God because it does not spring from a motive of love to Him. Only conduct that arises from love is worthy of the name of obedience.

To love God with all our heart and soul and mind, and to obey Him wholeheartedly and diligently are like the two sides of a coin. You cannot have one without the other. Fervency of worship on Sunday morning or in our private devotions is vain without an accompanying fervency in obedience to God. On the other hand, precise and exact obedience to the law of God is vain if it is not prompted by love for Him.

In his commentary on Matthew 22:37 John Calvin wrote,

> [Christ] means by this that only the free service of our wills is acceptable to Him. Ultimately the man who comes to obey God will love Him first. . . . Let us therefore learn that the love of God is the beginning of religion, for God will not have the forced obedience of men, but wishes their service to be free and spontaneous. . . . Lastly we learn that God does not linger over the outward sign of achievement but chiefly searches the inner disposition [motive], that from a good root good fruits may grow.[1]

My wife and I moved into a house that had an unfinished garage. Every time I went into the garage I saw the bare two-by-four studs and the black feltlike undersiding. After living for twenty years in a house with a finished garage, it was rather depressing to me. Our son came home for a visit and, learning of my feelings, volunteered to install insulation and drywall in the garage.

Dan had never worked with drywall before and had to learn by doing. The finished job, though very acceptable, was not quite what one would expect from a professional drywall installer. But I am more pleased than if a professional had done the work. Why? Because the job was done out of love. Dan didn't expect to get anything in return. He wasn't trying to earn favor or manipulate me. He just wanted to show his love. Now, every time I go into the garage I see the finished walls, but most of all, I see the love that went into them. Dan's motive was more important to me than his performance.

Our motive for obedience is just as important, probably more so, to God than the level of our performance. A person who struggles with some persistent sin but does so out of love for God is more pleasing to Him than the person who has no such struggle but is proud of his or her self-control. Of course, the person who obeys from a motive of love will be concerned about his or her performance. There will be a sincere desire and an earnest effort to please God in every area of life.

Other motives besides pride can taint our obedience. Probably next after pride is the motive of not wanting to feel guilty. This is especially true in areas of persistent sin. You have committed some particular sin many times before and you know well the guilt feelings that have followed the act. Your motive for struggling against that temptation is to avoid the guilt that follows, rather than to express love to God.

Another wrong motive is fear of the consequences of disobedience. In my book *Transforming Grace*, I told of a man who believed it was his duty to tithe (that is, give 10 percent of his income to God's work). When I asked him why he was so strict in the practice of tithing, he replied, "I'd be afraid not to." He was afraid God would punish him financially if he failed to tithe. His motive was not love but fear of perceived consequences.

Still another frequent motive is the desire to get something from God. It could be as subtle and silly as thinking that if I kneel to pray about a message I am to give, God will grant greater blessing than if I sit in my chair to pray. In using that example, I am not disparaging the act of kneeling to pray. I'm simply trying to illustrate how our deceitful hearts can lead us to do something good from some motive other than love to God.

GROWING IN LOVE

How then can we develop this love for God so that our obedience is prompted by love instead of some lesser motive? The Scripture gives us our first clue, or point of beginning, when it says, "We love because he first loved us" (1 John 4:19). Our love to God can only be a response to His love for us. If I do not believe God loves me, I cannot love Him. To love God, I must believe that He is for me, not against me (Romans 8:31), and that He accepts me as a son or a daughter, not a slave (Galatians 4:7).

What would keep us from believing that God loves us? The answer is a sense of guilt and condemnation because of our sin. Charles Hodge said,

> The great difficulty with many Christians is that they cannot persuade themselves that Christ (or God) loves them; and the reason why they cannot feel confident of the love of God, is, that they know they do not deserve his love, on the contrary, that they are in the highest degree unlovely. How can the infinitely pure God love those who are defiled with sin, who are proud, selfish, discontented, ungrateful, disobedient? This, indeed, is hard to believe.[2]

A tender conscience that is alert to sin, especially those "refined" sins such as pride, criticality, resentment, discontent, irritableness, and the like, is a great advantage in the pursuit of holiness, as it enables us to become aware of sins that lie deep beneath the level of external actions. But this same tender conscience can load us down with guilt, and when we are under that burden and sense of condemnation, it is difficult to love God or believe that He loves us.

James Fraser said, "But whilst the conscience retains the

charge of guilt, condemnation, and wrath, there cannot be purity, or sincerity of heart toward God, or sincerity of the love of God. Human nature is so formed, that it cannot love any object that is adverse and terrible to it."[3] What Fraser was essentially saying is that we cannot love God if we think we are under His judgment and condemnation.

This means that we must continually take those sins that our consciences accuse us of to the Cross and plead the cleansing blood of Jesus. It is only the blood of Christ that cleanses our consciences so that we may no longer feel guilty (Hebrews 9:14, 10:2). To paraphrase James Fraser, "The conscience once cleansed no longer retains a charge of guiltiness and of judgment for it. So there are two ways of having a good conscience. One is by not having transgressed; the other is by having the guilt taken away by the application of the blood of Jesus."[4]

When our sense of guilt is taken away because our consciences are cleansed by the blood of Christ, we are freed up to love Him with all our hearts and souls and minds. In fact, not only are we freed up, we are motivated in a positive sense to love Him in this wholehearted way. Our love will be spontaneous in an outpouring of gratitude to Him and fervent desire to obey Him.

Jesus said, "He who has been forgiven little loves little" (Luke 7:47). In the context of that statement He essentially said the converse is also true: Those who have been forgiven much love much. Therefore, we can say that the extent to which we realize and acknowledge our own sinfulness, and the extent to which we realize the total forgiveness and cleansing from those sins, will determine the measure of our love to God.

So if we want to grow in our love for God and in the acceptable obedience that flows out of that love, we must keep coming back to the Cross and the cleansing blood of Jesus Christ. That is why it is so important that we keep the gospel before us every day. Because we sin every day, and our consciences condemn us every day, we need the gospel every day.

FAITH AND LOVE

There is an inextricable link between faith and love. Without faith it is impossible to please God (Hebrews 11:6), and as we have seen, without love it is impossible to please God. But this love arises in our hearts only as we by faith lay hold of the great truths of the gospel. To do this, our faith must be constantly nourished by feeding on the gospel. That is why I stated in chapter 1 that the most important message we need to hear as believers is the gospel. It is not the only message; we do need to hear the requirements of discipleship. But the gospel is the most important, because it alone provides both the proper motive and the only enduring motivation to respond to our Lord's call to discipleship.

The Apostle Paul said in Galatians 5:6, "For in Christ Jesus neither circumcision nor uncircumcision has any value. The only thing that counts is faith expressing itself through love." As we by faith feed on the gospel, that faith will express itself in love; that is, in loving obedience to God. This is the very nature of faith.

Beginning with the next chapter we will consider some of the other disciplines we must practice that are important to the pursuit of holiness. But remember, none is more important than the discipline of continually feeding your soul on the great truth of the gospel.

John Owen was considered the prince of Puritan theologians. He wrote three masterful treatises on sin: *Of the Mortification of Sin in Believers; Of Temptation;* and *The Nature, Power, Deceit, and Prevalency of Indwelling Sin.* Those three volumes have been very influential in my own personal pursuit of holiness. He also wrote a book entitled *Communion with God* in which he made this statement: "The greatest sorrow and burden you can lay on the Father, the greatest unkindness you can do to him is not to believe that he loves you."[5]

Does that sentence surprise you? Would you have expected Owen to say that the greatest sorrow and burden we can lay on the Father is to commit some scandalous sin? Isn't that the way we tend to think of God, more as our Judge than as our Father? That is because we do not keep the gospel constantly before us. You can easily gather by the nature of his three treatises that John Owen was not soft on sin. In fact, his work on indwelling sin is very sobering—almost scary—as he exposes the nature, power, and deceitfulness of the sin that still resides in us. But Owen was more concerned that we keep before us the gospel: the love of God revealed in His Son Jesus Christ.

To the degree that we live with an abiding sense of His love for us in Christ, to that degree will we love God with all our heart and soul and mind. So as we turn our attention in the following chapters to the personal disciplines we need to practice in the pursuit of holiness, let us not put the gospel "on the shelf" of our lives. Let us review it daily, and in the joy that it brings, pursue these disciplines.

8

DEPENDENT DISCIPLINE

Unless the LORD builds the house,
its builders labor in vain.
Unless the LORD watches over the city,
the watchmen stand guard in vain.
PSALM 127:1

THINK OF YOURSELF SEATED in a jet passenger plane flying thirty-five thousand feet above the earth. Suppose (I know this can't happen in real life) the pilot were to say through the speaker system, "Folks, we're in real trouble. One of our wings is about to break off." Which one of the wings would you rather lose, the left or the right one? It's a silly question, isn't it? No plane can fly with just one wing. Multi-engined planes such as passenger airliners are designed to fly in an emergency mode with only one engine. But no plane can fly with just one wing; both are absolutely necessary.[1]

Visualize that aircraft as though you were looking down on it from above, as shown in the following illustration.

You see the fuselage, where you are sitting, the two wings, and the tail assembly. As you look at the two wings you see the words *dependence* on the left wing and *discipline* on the right wing. This airplane illustrates one of the most important principles in the Christian life. Just as the airplane must have both wings to fly, so we must exercise both discipline and dependence in the pursuit of holiness. Just as it is impossible for an airplane to fly with only one wing, so it is impossible for us to successfully pursue holiness with only dependence or discipline. We absolutely must have both.

Discipline, as I am now using it, refers to certain activities designed to train a person in a particular skill. The Apostle Paul exhorted Timothy to train himself, or discipline himself, to be godly (1 Timothy 4:7). In urging Timothy to train himself, he borrowed a term from the realm of athletics. The word originally referred to the training of young athletes for the competitive games of the day. It later came to include both mental and moral training. Paul used it to refer to spiritual training.

Note that Paul said to Timothy, "train yourself." In chapter 5, "Disciplined by Grace," we considered God's discipline of us, His spiritual child-training. Now we will be looking at the discipline of ourselves, the responsibilities we must shoulder to pursue holiness. But the point of the airplane illustration is that we must not try to carry out our responsibilities in our own strength and willpower. We must depend upon the Holy Spirit to enable us. At the same time we must not assume that we have no responsibility simply because we are dependent. God enables us to work, but He does not do the work for us.

WORK OR PRAY?

There are many instances in the Scriptures where the concepts of both dependence and responsibility appear in the same sentence or paragraph. For example, Psalm 127:1 says,

> Unless the LORD builds the house,
>   its builders labor in vain.
> Unless the LORD watches over the city,
>   the watchmen stand guard in vain.

The psalmist sees God so intimately involved in the building and watching that he says, "Unless the Lord *builds* the house, . . . unless the Lord *watches* over the city." He does not say, "Unless the Lord *helps* the builders and the watchmen," but unless the Lord builds and watches.

Yet it is just as obvious that the psalmist envisions the builders laboring to build the house and the watchmen standing guard over the city. The builders cannot put away their tools and go fishing and expect God to build the house. Neither can the watchmen retire to their beds and expect God to watch over the city. The builders must work, and the watchmen must stand guard, but they all must carry out their responsibilities in such total dependence on God that the psalmist speaks of *His* building and *His* watching.

Nehemiah, the wall-builder, understood well the principle of dependent discipline, the idea that we are both dependent and responsible. In his project of rebuilding the wall around Jerusalem, Nehemiah faced great opposition from certain enemies of the Jews. When the Jews had rebuilt the wall to half its height, the Scripture account says, "[These enemies] all plotted together to come and fight against Jerusalem and stir up trouble against it. But we prayed to our God and posted a guard day and night to meet this threat" (Nehemiah 4:8-9).

Note Nehemiah's response to the threatened attack. His people *prayed* and *posted* a guard. He recognized his dependence on God, but he also accepted his responsibility to work—that is, to stand guard.

Today, we would tend to divide into two camps. The more "spiritual" people would call an all-night prayer meeting. To them, posting a guard would be depending on human effort instead of God. The "practical" ones among us would get busy organizing the guard. They would do a fine job assigning everyone to the various watches of the night, but they would be too busy to pray. "What do you mean, have an all-night prayer meeting?" they would say. "We've got to man those guard posts."

Nehemiah and his people did both. They prayed and they also posted a guard. They recognized their dependence upon God, but they also understood that they were depending on Him to enable and help them, not to do their work for them.

Now there are instances in the Old Testament history of Israel where God miraculously intervened and actually fought the battle for Israel. (See 2 Chronicles 20 for an outstanding example of this.) But these instances are the exception, not the rule. However, and this is an important statement, there is not a single instance in New Testament teaching on holiness where we are taught to depend on the Holy Spirit without a corresponding exercise of discipline on our part.

Discipline is not necessarily a reliance on human effort, or as it is often called, a work "of the flesh." It can be, and unfortunately, often is. But when Paul urged Timothy to train, or discipline, himself to be godly, he certainly didn't envision a reliance on sheer human discipline and willpower. In fact in 2 Timothy 2:1, he urged Timothy to be strong in the grace—that is, the strength—that is in Christ Jesus. Yet Paul did exhort Timothy to discipline himself, not just "turn it all over to the Lord." We must have both wings of the airplane. We cannot fly with only one.

PAUL'S TESTIMONY

Consider the testimony of Paul in Philippians 4:11-13—

> I am not saying this because I am in need, for I have learned to be content whatever the circumstances. I know what it is to be in need, and I know what it is to have plenty. I have learned the secret of being content

> in any and every situation, whether well fed or hungry, whether living in plenty or in want. I can do everything through him who gives me strength.

Paul said he had *learned* to be content. He recognized it was his responsibility to be content, and that he needed to grow in that area of life. He didn't just turn it all over to the Lord and trust Him to do the work of being content. He worked at it. But he knew that he could be content only through the Lord, who gave him strength. Paul also realized that this strength from the Lord did not come to him as a "package sent from Heaven," as if Christ's strength were a commodity to be received. Rather, he knew it came as a result of his union with Christ. Because he was "in Christ" he was able by faith to rely upon Christ working in him through His Spirit.

We see another example of Paul's understanding of the principle of dependent discipline or responsibility in his description of his ministry. In Colossians 1:28-29, Paul said, "We proclaim him, admonishing and teaching everyone with all wisdom, so that we may present everyone perfect in Christ. To this end I labor, struggling with all his energy, which so powerfully works in me." In pursuit of his ministry Paul said he labored even to struggling. F. F. Bruce says the Greek word translated as "labor" in the *New International Version* is, "a strong word, denoting toil to the point of weariness or exhaustion."[2] The word *struggling* in Greek is the word *agonizomai*, from which we get our word *agonize*, and conveys the idea of an athlete straining to win the race.

So there is no question about the intensity of Paul's labors. He toiled to the point of weariness and he agonized like an athlete straining to break the tape. But he quickly adds, "with all his energy, which so powerfully works in me." Paul struggled, but he did so in the Lord's strength. He was disciplined in his ministry, but he was also dependent on the Lord. To return to our airplane illustration, he didn't try to fly with only one wing.

In Colossians 1:28-29, Paul was clearly writing about his

ministry, not his own pursuit of holiness. But he applied the same principle of dependent discipline to his personal life in learning contentment. He recognized his responsibility to discipline himself, to learn to be content, but he also recognized his dependence on the Holy Spirit.

THE PASSIVE APPROACH

We need to learn this scriptural principle that the Holy Spirit works in us to enable us to live lives pleasing to God. He does not do the work for us; rather, He enables us to do the work. We often use the expression "Let the Lord live His life through me." I am personally uncomfortable with this expression because it suggests a passivity on our part. He does not live His life through me. Rather, as I depend on Him, He enables *me* to live a life pleasing to Him.

Some years ago when I was following this more passive approach, which did indeed seem more spiritual to me at the time, I was struggling to love a Christian brother. One evening God really dealt with me about my lack of love, and I sensed God was saying to me through a thought planted in my mind, "If I love him, can you?" I responded, "Lord, I can't, but I'm willing for You to love him through me."

What happened? Over time my attitude toward this brother did change. In fact, we became good friends. Did Jesus then love him through me? No, He enabled *me* to love the man. We are not passive in the pursuit of holiness. We are the ones who love. We are the ones who clothe ourselves with compassion, kindness, humility, gentleness, and patience (Colossians 3:12). But we do this in utter dependence on Him who gives us strength.

This is far more than an issue of mere semantics. It is a difference in our understanding of how God works in us. The essence of the passive view (in fairness to those who teach this view of sanctification, they would call it a "faith" approach, not a passive approach) is summed up in a statement that goes something like this: Man's part is to trust; God's part is to work. The believer can do nothing but trust, while the God in whom he or she trusts does the work.

It is the idea that we can do *nothing* but trust that is particularly troubling to me. I believe that the psalmist—and Nehemiah and Paul—would say, "Man's part is to trust *and* work. God's part is to *enable* the man or woman to do the work." Or perhaps it is more helpful to say, "Our part is to work, but to do so in reliance upon God to enable us to work." God's work does not make our effort unnecessary, but rather makes it effective. Paul did not say, "Christ shows contentment through me." Rather, he said, "I have learned to be content through Him who gives me strength."

I am loath to take issue with many godly Christians who believe and teach this more passive approach. I do so with great reluctance and, I trust, with equal humility and love. But I embraced this teaching for several years, and with great difficulty came to what I now believe to be the biblical teaching on dependence and responsibility.

One of the Puritan writers who helped me most to understand the biblical relationship of dependence and discipline was John Owen. Since Owen's seventeenth-century writing style was somewhat ponderous, let me paraphrase a few sentences from him on the relationship of grace (God's divine enablement) and our responsibility, which he calls our duty:

> Let us consider what regard we ought to have to our own duty and to the grace of God. Some would separate these things as inconsistent. If holiness be our duty, they would say, there is no room for grace; and if it be the result of grace there is no place for duty. But our duty and God's grace are nowhere opposed in the matter of sanctification; for the one absolutely supposes the other. We cannot perform our duty without the grace of God; nor does God give his grace for any other purpose than that we may perform our duty.[3]

There is no question that we are responsible to pursue holiness with all the intensity that the word *pursue* implies.

Every moral imperative in the Bible addresses itself to our responsibility to discipline ourselves unto godliness. We are not just to turn it all over to the Lord and let Him live His life through us. Rather, we are to love one another; we are to put to death the misdeeds of the body; we are to put off the old man and put on the new man.

If we are to make any progress in the pursuit of holiness, we must assume our responsibility to discipline or train ourselves. But we are to do all this in total dependence on the Holy Spirit to work in us and strengthen us with the strength that is in Christ.

Sometimes we don't sense that we are experiencing His strength. Instead we experience deep, agonizing failure. We may even weep over our sins and wonder why the Holy Spirit doesn't come to our aid and strengthen us against the onslaught of temptation. We identify with Paul when he said, "I do not understand what I do. For what I want to do I do not do, but what I hate I do" (Romans 7:15).

Why doesn't the Holy Spirit always strengthen us? The answer may be one or more of several reasons. He may be letting us see the sinfulness of our own hearts. Or He may be causing us to realize how weak we are in ourselves and how dependent on Him we really are. Perhaps He is curbing a tendency toward spiritual pride and causing us to grow in humility. Whatever the reason, which we may never know, our responsibility is to utterly depend on Him. He sovereignly and with infinite wisdom determines how best to respond to our dependence.

THE SELF-DISCIPLINE APPROACH
Despite my concern about the so-called passive approach to holiness, I am just as concerned about the self-discipline approach. There is no doubt that disciplined people, both believers and unbelievers, can effect change in themselves. Even as I work on this chapter, I am reading an excellent secular book on personal growth. I have no doubt that people who apply the principles expounded by the author see

change in their lives. I hope to see some myself.

A major temptation in the self-discipline approach to holiness, however, is to rely on a regimen of spiritual disciplines instead of on the Holy Spirit. I believe in spiritual disciplines. I seek to practice them, and we are going to be considering some that especially relate to the pursuit of holiness in the remaining chapters of this book. But those disciplines are not the source of our spiritual strength. The Lord Jesus Christ is, and it is the ministry of the Holy Spirit to apply His strength in our lives. To paraphrase Paul's statement in 1 Corinthians 3:7, we can plant and we can water, but we cannot make things grow. Only the Holy Spirit can do that.

The truth is, we must plant and we must water if we are to make progress in holiness, but only the Holy Spirit can change us more and more into the likeness of Jesus. Our problem is that we tend to *depend* upon our planting and our watering rather than on the Lord.

Since Paul used a metaphor from farming—planting and watering—let's pursue that illustration. In the business of farming there are certain things farmers must do, but there are two things they cannot do. We can chart what they can and must do versus what they cannot do in the following manner:

Can and Must Do	Cannot Do
Plow	Make grow
Plant	Control weather
Fertilize	
Irrigate	
Cultivate	
Harvest	

There are six things farmers must do and only two things they cannot do. They can even to a degree circumvent the weather by irrigating in case of drought. But the one thing they absolutely cannot do is the most critical of all. Without the life that makes things grow, all their disciplines of farming are useless. Now typical farmers, unless they are godly believers, will concentrate on the things they must do and will tend to take for granted the life in the seed that makes it grow. They will put all their confidence in the performance of their duties, not in God, who makes things grow. As far as they are concerned, their success depends on themselves.

As in the case of farming, God has ordained certain disciplines or practices that are necessary in order to grow in holiness. We must observe these or we will not grow, just as farmers will not produce a crop if they do not perform their duties. There is one thing, however, we cannot do. We cannot make ourselves grow. But just as typical farmers put their confidence in the performance of their duties, so we believers who take seriously our responsibility for holiness tend to put our confidence in the performance of our disciplines. Like farmers, we take for granted the spiritual life that makes us grow.

John Owen is helpful to us at this point also, and again for the convenience of the reader, I will paraphrase. Owen wrote, "The actual aid and internal operation of the Spirit of God is necessary to produce every holy act of our minds, wills, and emotions in every duty whatsoever. Notwithstanding the power or ability that believers have received by the principle of new life implanted at salvation, they still stand in need of the divine enablement of the Holy Spirit in every single act or duty toward God."[4] So even though we have been given a new heart and the principle of spiritual life, that new life needs to be continually nourished and sustained by the Holy Spirit. It does not operate on its own.

Jonathan Edwards, the great philosopher-theologian (and a pastor as well) of colonial America, compiled a series of seventy resolutions to govern his own spiritual disciplines and conduct. Talk about spiritual discipline! Edwards's resolutions would make most of our present-day disciplines look like spiritual kindergarten. But at the beginning of his list of written resolutions he wrote these words: "Being sensible that I am unable to do any thing without God's help, I do humbly entreat him, by his grace, to enable me to keep these Resolutions, so far as they are agreeable to his will, for Christ's sake."[5] Edwards was disciplined, but he was also dependent.

I'm sure those of us who tend toward the self-discipline school of holiness agree with John Owen and Jonathan Edwards that we are dependent on the enabling power of the Holy Spirit. We believe it and we give lip service to it, but do we practice it? Do we each day and throughout the day acknowledge our dependence on Him? Or do we in fact seek to pursue holiness in the strength of our own willpower?

We all know those familiar words of Jesus, "Apart from me you can do nothing" (John 15:5). In theory we believe them, but in practice we tend to live as if we *can* do some things. All of us have certain areas of morality and ethics in which we feel fairly confident. We tend to rely on our own goodness in those areas; we don't sense the need of the Holy Spirit's aid. But Jesus said, "Apart from me . . . nothing." We cannot do anything spiritually good apart from the working of His Spirit within us. If we are going to make any progress in becoming more like Christ, we must learn to rely on the Holy Spirit rather than on our own virtues and abilities.

THE DISCIPLINE OF PRAYER

How then can we grow in a conscious sense of dependence on Christ? Through the discipline of prayer. Prayer is the tangible expression of our dependence. We may assent to the fact that we are dependent on Christ, but if our prayer life is meager or perfunctory, we thereby deny it. We are in effect saying we can handle most of our spiritual life with our own self-discipline and our perceived innate goodness. Or perhaps we are saying we are not even committed to the pursuit of holiness.

The writer of Psalm 119 teaches us about the discipline

of prayer in the pursuit of holiness. We usually think of this psalm as the psalm of the Word of God, since God's Word is mentioned by various names in all but four of its 176 verses. But it is more accurately an expression of the psalmist's ardent desire for and commitment to the pursuit of holiness. Twenty-two times the psalmist prays to God for help in obeying His law. Verses 33-37 are a good example:

> Teach me, O LORD, to follow your decrees;
>> then I will keep them to the end.
> Give me understanding, and I will keep your law
>> and obey it with all my heart.
> Direct me in the path of your commands,
>> for there I find delight.
> Turn my heart toward your statutes
>> and not toward selfish gain.
> Turn my eyes away from worthless things;
>> preserve my life according to your word.

The psalmist wants God to teach him, to give him understanding, and to direct him in the paths of God's commands. He also wants God to work directly in his heart, turning his heart toward His statutes and his eyes away from worthless things. But the psalmist also exercised spiritual discipline. Notice his discipline with regard to the Word of God:

> I have hidden your word in my heart
>> that I might not sin against you.
> Praise be to you, O LORD;
>> teach me your decrees.
> With my lips I recount
>> all the laws that come from your mouth.
> I rejoice in following your statutes
>> as one rejoices in great riches.
> I meditate on your precepts
>> and consider your ways.

> I delight in your decrees;
>> I will not neglect your word.
>>> (Psalm 119:11-16)

The psalmist stored up God's Word in his heart. He recounted it to others, he rejoiced in obeying it, he meditated on it, he delighted in it, and he did not neglect it. The psalmist was not only a man of discipline but also a man of prayer. His discipline did not cause him to neglect prayer for God to work, nor did his prayer cause him to neglect his own work. He practiced discipline *and* dependence.

THE EXAMPLE OF NEHEMIAH

Our prayers of dependence should be of two types: planned periods of prayer and unplanned, spontaneous prayer. We see both of these beautifully illustrated for us in the life of Nehemiah and recorded for us in chapters 1 and 2 of that book. Nehemiah was one of the Jews in exile and was cupbearer to the Persian king Artaxerxes. The book begins with Nehemiah learning of the sad state of affairs of the Jews back in Judah and the fact that the wall of Jerusalem was broken down and its gates burned with fire. Upon hearing this, Nehemiah sat down and wept. Then he fasted and prayed for a period of several months (Nehemiah 1).

The Scripture account doesn't indicate this, but we can assume that Nehemiah set aside a certain time or times of the day during which he earnestly besought God for the welfare of Jerusalem. After all, he was the king's cupbearer and, as such, would have had official duties to perform. So, most likely he would have had to schedule his times of prayer around his daily duties, just as we have to do. Since he prayed over a period of several months, we can describe this part of Nehemiah's prayer life as *planned, protracted, persevering* prayer. It was planned because it was made a part of his daily schedule, protracted because it extended over a period of several months, and persevering because he continued to pray until God answered.

One day, after several months of praying, when Nehemiah brought the king's wine to him, the king noticed that Nehemiah's face was sad. Up to this time Nehemiah had concealed his sadness of heart for his countrymen and the condition of their beloved city, Jerusalem. But now the king inquired about the cause of his sadness, and Nehemiah explained it to him (Nehemiah 2:1-3).

Then King Artaxerxes said, "What is it you want?" (verse 4). The moment of crisis had arrived. Now Nehemiah must lay before the king his request to go to Jerusalem and rebuild its wall. But before he replied, Nehemiah "prayed to the God of heaven, and [he] answered the king" (verses 4-5). Obviously the king was not aware of Nehemiah's quick, silent prayer. It was probably something like, "Lord, help me to speak. Give me favor in the king's heart." Nehemiah sent up this quick, silent prayer to Heaven even as he was opening his mouth to speak to the king. In contrast to his planned, protracted, persevering prayer over the previous few months, this prayer was *unplanned, short,* and *spontaneous.*

Both types of prayer were needed in Nehemiah's situation. Each gave validity to the other. Nehemiah didn't presume on God by waiting until that eventful day in the king's court to pray. He saw a need, and he persisted in prayer until God answered.

At the same time, Nehemiah didn't plunge ahead to answer the king without first praying quickly and silently. He didn't presume that because he had been praying for several months he didn't need to pray at that time. He was very conscious of his total dependence on God, so his quick, silent prayer was a reflex action rather than a planned one.

We can learn from Nehemiah's example how to pray for ourselves in the pursuit of holiness. Like Nehemiah, we need to set aside time each day for *planned, protracted, persevering* prayer. We need to lay before the Lord any areas of persistent sin in our lives: sins such as gossip; irritability; impatience; lack of love; impure thoughts; and undisciplined, wandering eyes. These sins need to be the object of earnest prayer that God would work in us and enable us to deal with them. Note that I said, *enable us*. We are the ones who must deal with these sins, but the Holy Spirit must enable us to do it.

In Romans 8:13 the Apostle Paul wrote, "But if by the Spirit you put to death the misdeeds of the body, you will live." Note again the dependent discipline. There is the discipline of putting to death the sins of the body that we will consider in detail in chapter 11, but we do this "by the Spirit." This means continual, fervent prayer for the work of the Holy Spirit to enable us to do what is our duty to do. As John Murray said, "The believer is not endowed with a reservoir of strength from which he draws. It is always 'by the Spirit' that each sanctified and sanctifying activity is exercised."[6]

It is precisely because we are not endowed with a reservoir of strength that we need to pray daily for the Spirit's enabling work in us. Holiness requires continual effort on our part and continual nourishing and strengthening by the Holy Spirit. Unless you *plan* to pray, however, and set aside a specific *time* to do it, you will find that you will not carry out your good intentions. So if you do not already have this practice, why not stop and make your plan now? I also find it helpful to write down on paper (for my eyes only) the specific sins I need help to deal with and the specific virtues of Christian character in which, as far as I can tell, I most need to grow.

In addition to prayer about sins in our lives and areas of character in which we need to grow, it is also good to pray that we will be kept from temptation (Matthew 6:13) and that we will be alert to and not be blindsided by temptation when it does come. Finally, in our planned time of prayer, it is good to pray along the lines of Hebrews 13:21, that God will work in us what is pleasing to Him, for He knows far better than we what really needs to happen in our lives at any given time.

Then like Nehemiah, we need those unplanned, short, spontaneous prayers. We need them throughout the day as we face temptations to sin and as we encounter circumstances in which we need help to display godly character. Whatever the situation, a simple, quick "Lord, help me" focuses our dependence upon God instead of our own willpower and brings the Spirit's aid to us. He does withhold His aid when we forget our need of it and do not ask Him for it. So we need those short, spontaneous prayers throughout the day, both to help us cultivate a sense of our dependence on Christ and to receive His aid that He sends through His Spirit.

THE SIN OF SELF-SUFFICIENCY

I believe that one of the chief characteristics of our sinful nature, or "flesh" as it is called in most Bible translations, is an attitude of independence toward God. Even when we know and agree that we are dependent on Him, we tend out of habit to act independently. It is part of "the evil I do not want to do—this I keep on doing" (Romans 7:19) syndrome that clings so tightly to us. Undoubtedly, one of the reasons God allows us to fall before temptation so often is to teach us experientially that we really are dependent on Him to enable us to grow in holiness.

One of the best ways, apart from those painful experiences of failure, to learn dependence is to develop the discipline of prayer. This forces us in a tangible way to acknowledge our dependence on the Holy Spirit. This is true because, for whatever else we may say about prayer, it is a recognition of our own helplessness and absolute dependence on God.

It is this admission of helplessness and dependence that is so repugnant to our sinful spirit of self-sufficiency. And if we are naturally prone by temperament to be disciplined, it is even more difficult to acknowledge that we are dependent on Christ and His Spirit instead of on our self-discipline.

Remember, however, that to become holy is to become like the Lord Jesus. And He Himself said, "By myself I can do nothing" (John 5:30). He was completely dependent on the

Father, and He freely and willingly acknowledged it. His dependence was not reluctant; it was wholehearted—enthusiastic, even—because He knew that we are created to be dependent on God. So if we want to become holy we must pursue, not a spirit of independence, but a spirit of dependence. And one of the best means God has given us for doing this is the discipline of prayer.

Think of the two wings of the airplane: *discipline* and *dependence*. Do they exist in equal proportion in your life? Actually, we haven't even begun to get into the disciplines yet, except for the disciplines of beholding Christ in the gospel and, now, prayer. Before we are finished, we'll be looking at several more, and you will end up with a list of about six disciplines on the "discipline" wing of your airplane. But remember the farming illustration. There were six disciplines that farmers must perform, and only one thing they absolutely could not do. But that one thing was the most essential of all. So you may end up with six disciplines on that wing and only the one word, *dependence*, on the other wing. But dependence is the most vital of all and provides the essential balance to the sum of the disciplines.

Dependence is not simply one of a list of several disciplines. Rather, it gives life and vitality to them. Just as the principle of life that makes the seed grow gives fruition to all of the farmers' efforts, so the enabling of the Holy Spirit within us gives fruition to our disciplines. Therefore, as we proceed to study the disciplines that are necessary to pursue holiness, keep in mind that dependence on the Holy Spirit should permeate them all.

9

THE DISCIPLINE OF COMMITMENT

I have taken an oath and confirmed it,
that I will follow your righteous laws.
PSALM 119:106

A CARTOON IN A recent edition of our daily paper showed a man ready to leap from the ledge of a high-rise apartment building with a suicide note in his hand but with a parachute strapped to his back. His wife, leaning out of the window, says to him, "Just can't make a commitment to anything can you, Larry?"

Although intended to be humorous, the cartoon nevertheless made a very telling statement about our present-day society. The time-honored virtue of commitment, once so highly esteemed, has fallen on hard times. Like Larry in the cartoon, people seem averse to commit themselves to anything these days.

One notable exception to society's general aversion to commitment is in the lives of Olympic-class athletes. It is obvious that no one ever reaches the Olympic Games without a commitment to the rigorous training required to reach that level of performance. It is not without reason that, when the Apostle Paul urged Timothy to train himself to be godly

(1 Timothy 4:7), he used a word from the athletic world of that time. Paul knew that training in godliness, or the pursuit of holiness, or any other spiritual pursuit would require that same high level of commitment. If we ourselves hope to make any progress in the pursuit of holiness, commitment is absolutely essential. One reason we do not see more progress in holiness in our lives is because we have for the most part lost sight of the necessity of commitment.

COMMIT YOURSELF TO GOD

When Paul turned his attention from his masterful exposition of the gospel in Romans chapters 1–11 to practical issues of Christian living, the first thing he did was call for commitment.

> Therefore, I urge you, brothers, in view of God's mercy, to offer your bodies as living sacrifices, holy and pleasing to God—this is your spiritual act of worship. (Romans 12:1)

As we look at Paul's call to commitment, we can see one obvious difference between the commitment of the Olympic athlete and the commitment Paul called for. The athlete's commitment is to himself or herself or perhaps to the team. The commitment Paul urged upon us is to God. Commit yourself to God. Offer your body to Him as a living sacrifice, holy and pleasing to Him.

When we commit ourselves to the pursuit of holiness, we need to ensure that our commitment is actually to God, not simply to a holy lifestyle or a set of moral values. The people of my parent's generation were generally honest, chaste, sober, and thrifty. They were committed to those values, but they were not necessarily committed to God. Many of them were outstanding moralists and even church people, but they were not committed to God. *They were committed to their values, not to God.*

As believers we need to be careful that we do not make a similar mistake. We can be committed to a set of Christian values or to a lifestyle of discipleship without being committed to God Himself. But Paul said, offer yourselves to God, and in doing that commit yourselves to the pursuit of holiness in order to please Him.

We should not seek holiness in order to feel good about ourselves, or to blend in with our Christian peer group, or to avoid the sense of shame and guilt that follows the committing of persistent sin in our lives. Far too often our concern with sin arises from how it makes us feel. Sinful habits, sometimes called "besetting sins," cause us to feel defeated, and we don't like to be defeated in anything, whether it's in a game of Ping-Pong or in our struggle with sin.

I once spoke at a retreat on the importance of putting on Christlike character while at the same time seeking to put off sinful habits. After my message four or five people came to me asking for personal help in dealing with some particular sin in their lives. That was all well and good, but it struck me that no one came asking for help in putting on any Christlike virtues. As I pondered the possible reason for this, I realized that sinful habits make us feel guilty and defeated. The absence of Christlike character usually doesn't have a similar effect on us, so there is less motivation to seek change in our lives.

We need to work at ensuring that our commitment to holiness is a commitment to God, not to our own self-esteem. Frederick W. Faber, a nineteenth-century British writer, showed great insight into this tendency. Again, for the sake of clarity I will paraphrase:

> When we sin we are more vexed at the lowering of our self-esteem than we are grieved at God's dishonor. We are surprised and irritated at our own lack of self-control in subjecting ourselves to unworthy habits. . . . The first cause of this is self-love, which is unable to stand the disappointment of not seeing ourselves in time of trial come out beautiful, erect, and admirable.[1]

The Apostle Paul had already called for a commitment to God in Romans 6:13. There he wrote, "Do not offer the parts of your body to sin, as instruments of wickedness, but rather offer yourselves to God, as those who have been brought from death to life; and offer the parts of your body to him as instruments of righteousness." In that verse Paul drew a sharp contrast between offering the parts of our body to sin as instruments of wickedness and offering them to God as instruments of righteousness. But the basis for this diametric change of commitment is the offering of *ourselves*—our entire being—to God. We cannot control what our eyes look at, what our mouth speaks, or what our hands and feet do, if our whole being, including our mind and heart, is not committed to God.

The word *offer* in Romans 12:1 has the idea of a decisive, once-for-all dedication or commitment. We are to put our bodies at God's disposal with the same finality that an Israelite would bring his animal sacrifice to the Temple to be slain and offered up to God. At the same time, it is to be a living sacrifice, signifying a constant dedication or a perpetual sacrifice never to be neglected or recalled. So the commitment to holiness must be a decisive commitment that is continually reaffirmed.

NO EXCEPTIONS

Commitment to the pursuit of holiness, then, is first of all a commitment to God to pursue a way of life that is pleasing to Him. In short, it is commitment to a life of obedience. Such a commitment must allow for no exceptions, no secret sins we want to hold onto, no sinful habits we are unwilling to give up. *We must make it our aim not to sin.*

This doesn't mean we can arrive at sinless perfection in this life, for even our best deeds are stained with sin. But it does mean that our firm intention must be to not sin willfully. We will study the issue of choices in the face of temptation in chapter 11, but for now we need to know that commitment to a life of holiness without exception is a requirement for consistently making the right choices. There is no point in praying for God's help in the face of temptation if we have not made a commitment to obedience without exception.

The psalmist said,

> I have taken an oath and confirmed it,
> that I will follow your righteous laws.
> (Psalm 119:106)

He felt so strongly about his commitment to obedience that he took an oath that he would follow God's righteous laws. An oath, in this context, is a solemn calling on God to witness that the person sincerely intends to do what he or she says. It is a declaration or promise to fulfill a pledge. It is a commitment of the highest level. The psalmist not only took an oath but confirmed it. He wanted to make his commitment as strong as he possibly could.

The Puritan pastor and writer Stephen Charnock commented on this verse: "Frequently renew settled and holy resolutions. A soldier unresolved to fight may easily be defeated. . . . The weakness of our graces, the strength of our temptations, and the diligence of our spiritual enemies, require strong resolutions."[2]

I have already referred in chapter 8 to Jonathan Edwards's seventy resolutions. One of his resolutions was, "*Resolved, that I will live so, as I shall wish I had done when I come to die.*"[3] Edwards wanted no exceptions in his commitment to the pursuit of holiness. He knew that at the time of death the little dalliances with sin that seem so attractive in time of health would become cause of deep regret.

How do we respond to such a challenge to commitment; to present our bodies as living sacrifices; to, as it were, take an oath to obey God's righteous laws; to resolve to allow no exceptions to our obedience? I suspect all of us think first of the impossibility of totally keeping such a commitment. And we are reluctant to make a commitment we know we will not keep. But the question still persists, Are we willing to make that our aim, our goal in life?

Remember the analogy of "cruise-control" obedience versus "race-driver" obedience? Are we willing to commit ourselves to the race-driver approach, or will we settle for the mediocrity of merely avoiding scandalous sin? Are we willing to deal with the "refined" sins in our lives and the so-called little sins that we may consider unimportant? Are we willing to commit ourselves to a goal of obedience without exception? Such a commitment is necessary if we are to make progress in the pursuit of holiness.

WHAT ARE YOUR INTENTIONS?

William Law in his classic, *A Serious Call to a Devout and Holy Life*, was at one point writing about profanity, or swearing as he called it. He said, "Now the reason of common swearing is this, it is because men have not so much as the intention to please God in all their actions."[4] How about us today? Is it our intention to please God in all our actions? That is the commitment Paul called on us to make when he urged us to offer our bodies as living sacrifices to God.

Law continued,

> And if you will here stop, and ask yourself, why you are not as [holy] as the primitive Christians were, your own heart will tell you, that it is neither through ignorance, nor inability, but purely because you never thoroughly intended it. . . . This doctrine does not suppose, that we have no need of divine grace, or that it is in our own power to make ourselves perfect. It only supposes, that through the [lack] of a sincere intention of pleasing God in all our actions, we fall into such irregularities of life, as by the ordinary means of grace, we should have power to avoid.[5]

It is the intention to please God in all our actions that is the key to commitment to a life of holiness. If we do not make such a commitment to obedience without exception, we will constantly find ourselves making exceptions. We will have a "just one more time" syndrome in our lives. But the truth is, the "one more time" manner of thinking undermines our commitment. Every time we give in to a temptation, even though it may seem small and insignificant to us, we make it easier to give in the next time.

Sin has a tendency to exert an ever-increasing power on us if it is not resisted on every occasion. The Apostle Paul wrote in Romans 6:19, "Just as you used to offer the parts of your body in slavery to impurity and to ever-increasing wickedness, so now offer them in slavery to righteousness leading to holiness." We will study this scripture in more detail in chapter 11, but for now notice the phrase "ever-increasing wickedness." Paul was referring to this ability and tendency of sin to exert a greater and greater pull on us as we give in to each temptation.

It does not matter whether the sin to which we are tempted is seemingly small or large. The principle we are looking at—that saying yes to any temptation weakens our commitment to resist sin—works in either case.

Just as we need to make a commitment not to sin willfully, so we need to make a commitment to put on or clothe ourselves with the positive virtues of Christian character. Remember that Paul said, "Clothe yourselves with compassion, kindness, humility, gentleness and patience" (Colossians 3:12). We saw in chapter 2 that there are at least twenty-seven of these positive character traits that we are to seek after. What is our intention regarding them? If we want to be like Christ in His character, we must commit ourselves to putting on His virtues.

It is not enough to stop cheating on our income tax returns; we must also learn to share with those in need. It is not enough to avoid being bitter against those who have wronged us; we need to forgive as God has forgiven us. It is not enough to pray that God will enable us to deal with a volatile temper; we must also ask Him to help us put on compassion and kindness.

And just as we need to make a commitment to deal with all sin in our lives without exception, so we need to make a commitment to be just as diligent in putting on the fruit of the Spirit. Again, the observations of William Law are helpful to us in this regard.

> Again, let a Tradesman but have this intention, and it will make him a saint in his shop; his everyday business will be a course of wise and reasonable actions, made holy to God, by being done in obedience to his will and pleasure. . . . He will therefore consider, not what arts, or methods, or application will soonest make him richer and greater than his brothers, or remove him from a shop to a life of state and pleasure; but he will consider what arts, what methods, what application can make worldly business most acceptable to God, and make a life of trade a life of holiness, devotion, and piety. This will be the temper and spirit of every tradesman; he cannot stop short of these degrees of piety, whenever it is his intention to please God in all his actions, as the best and happiest thing in the world.[6]

Law was, of course, applying the principle of "intentions," or as I would say, commitment, to society as it existed in his day, particularly in the realm of business. The tradesman he referred to had a one-man business; he was a shoemaker, a tanner, a tailor, or something else. And Law was saying that the tradesman should commit himself to operate his business, not in such a way as to make the most money, but in such a way as to be most pleasing to God. The principle, then, is that we should commit ourselves to doing everything we do, not in the way that might seem to bring us the most gain or best accomplish our personal objective, but in the way that will be most pleasing to God.

This principle applies to the way a student approaches his or her studies, to the way we do our shopping and buying, to the way we compete in games and athletics, to the way we decorate our houses and keep our lawns, and even to the way we drive.

The city where we live attracts a lot of visitors in the summer, and the road I used to drive to our office is frequently crowded with tourists at that time. Being unfamiliar with the city and sometimes unsure of their directions, tourists often tend to drive more slowly than we "locals." It is easy in such a situation to become impatient with them and to show that impatience in the way we drive. Sometimes after I had "whipped around" someone so I could get on to work, I found myself hoping that person did not then see me turning into the driveway of a Christian organization.

The truth is, though, God knows I am a Christian and He knows I work for a Christian organization. If I would be ashamed to have a tourist identify my impatient driving with a Christian, how much more should I be ashamed before God. After all, He is the one I have committed myself to, to seek to please in all my thoughts and words and actions. So our commitment to pursue holiness must embrace every area of life and must include both the significant and the seemingly insignificant things we do. It must be a commitment both to put off the way of life of the old self and to put on the virtues of the new self.

SPECIFIC COMMITMENTS

In addition to an overall commitment to pursue holiness in every area of life, I find it helpful to make specific commitments in areas where we are particularly vulnerable or prone to sin. For example, if we are prone to gossip or to speak critically of others, it is helpful to make a specific commitment to stop those practices. We will consider *how* to do that in the next two chapters, but for now, I want to emphasize the value of identifying those areas where we are most vulnerable to sin—either in what we do (gossip, etc.) or in what we fail to do (loving our wives as Christ loved the

Church, etc.)—and then to make specific commitments in those areas.

We find two examples of specific commitments in the lives of Job and Daniel. Job's commitment was in regard to lustful looks, a temptation that is common to men and one that needs to be guarded against every day. Job said,

> "I made a covenant with my eyes
>   not to look lustfully at a girl." (Job 31:1)

Job was acknowledged by God Himself as a man who was "blameless and upright, a man who fears God and shuns evil" (Job 1:8). Yet Job found it helpful to single out this specific area of temptation and make a commitment regarding it, a commitment he described as, "making a covenant with my eyes."

Daniel's commitment was to not eat food that would violate the dietary laws God had established for the nation of Israel. Daniel was among those of the Jewish nation who had been taken into exile in Babylon, and he was selected, along with other young Israelites from the royal family and the nobility, to be trained to enter the Babylonian king's service. During their time of training they were to eat of the same food that was served at the king's table. This was a problem, however, because the king's food would include items forbidden by God for the Jews to eat.

Daniel 1:8 reads, "But Daniel resolved not to defile himself with the royal food and wine, and he asked the chief official for permission not to defile himself this way." Daniel made a specific commitment not to sin against God by violating the Jewish dietary laws. The account in Scripture suggests that he did this in full knowledge of the possibility that violating the king's command might result in his losing his head. (See verse 10. If the official was fearful of losing his head over Daniel's diet, we can assume Daniel was in danger of losing his also.)

Job's temptation to look lustfully at a girl arose from the

sinfulness of his own heart. Daniel's temptation came from the environment or circumstances in which he found himself. *We are vulnerable to both kinds of temptations.* Some arise from indwelling sin that still resides in our hearts; others come as a result of the environment in which we live or work.

An automobile dealer became a believer some years ago. At that time there was a widespread practice among dealerships to turn back the odometers of cars taken as trade-ins. If a car's odometer showed forty thousand miles, for example, it might be turned back to only thirty thousand. As soon as this man became a Christian he realized that was an unethical practice, so he made a commitment to stop. He did this, of course, in full awareness that such a commitment would put him at a disadvantage relative to other dealers who were still turning back odometers. The temptation to continue an unethical practice, however, was there because of the particular business environment in which he operated.

An executive in a large company became convicted about "padding" his travel expense accounts. But, as he said to me, "the problem is, everyone in the company does it." He knew that he would be under great pressure, because, if he turned in an honest expense report, his peers would look bad by comparison. But he committed himself to act honestly in that situation.

Here are two examples of businessmen who faced the temptation to continue a sinful practice because of the environment in which they operated. It seems that almost everyone who does business of any kind in our current social climate will sooner or later face ethical temptations. Even though I work with a Christian organization, I have had an air-travel agent suggest to me ways by which I could evade certain ticketing regulations so as to avoid a higher ticket price. People will help you compromise your integrity if you have not already made a commitment to be absolutely honest in your business dealings.

There is a very interesting and challenging insight about

Job and Daniel in Ezekiel 14:14. In the context of that verse God was speaking to the prophet Ezekiel about His judgment upon a country that sins against Him. In verse 14 God said, "Even if these three men—Noah, Daniel and Job—were in it, they could save only themselves by their righteousness." God was saying His anger would be so aroused that, unlike the time when He told Abraham that He would spare Sodom and Gomorrah if He found ten righteous people in them, He would not spare that country even if Noah, Daniel, and Job were in it. They would save only themselves by their righteousness.

God wanted to make a point that even the presence of three righteous men would not spare a country from His wrath. And to make His point He reached back across all the history of humankind up to that time and selected the names of three men who would be noted for their righteousness. Two of them, Noah and Job, were from antiquity. Daniel was a contemporary of Ezekiel during the seventy years of exile. But two of these three men provide our brief case studies about making specific commitments. The lesson to us is, if Job and Daniel, righteous as they were, needed to make commitments regarding specific areas of temptation, how much more do we.

I urge you, before you finish this chapter, to stop and list any areas of temptation wherein you need to make a specific commitment. Do you need to make a covenant with your eyes about what you look at, or with your mouth about what you say, or with your mind about what you think? Is there a particular temptation, or even a sinful practice, that arises in your work, school, or professional environment that needs a commitment to fortify you against it? Write these commitments down on paper only for your eyes so you can review them and pray over them daily.

Perhaps there is a particular area in your marriage or in your relationship with your children, or your parents, or even a friend, or with an associate at work, where you are not demonstrating the Spirit's fruit of love, patience, or kindness. Do you need to make a commitment that, in dependence on the Holy Spirit to enable you, you will seek to display that particular "fruit" toward that individual? If so, I urge you to make such a commitment. In fact, you may find you will need to make several commitments—sins to put off or avoid and Christlike traits to put on. If you do not commit yourself to the pursuit of holiness in these specific areas of your life, you will find a tendency to vacillate in the face of these temptations.

MOTIVE AND MOTIVATION

I suspect the overall flavor of this chapter may seem too rigorous and even legalistic to some people. "Who," they may ask, "can possibly keep such a commitment to a pursuit of holiness without exception for even some 'small' sins? And if there are no exceptions, is there any place for grace? Is God really this strict?"

Yes, God really is this strict, because He cannot compromise His holiness the least bit. His goal is to conform us to the likeness of His Son, and Jesus was completely without sin, though He was tempted in every way that we are (Hebrews 4:15). No, we cannot, or perhaps will not, keep these commitments perfectly, but keeping them perfectly should at least be our aim. In a battle, some soldiers will always be hit, but every one of them makes it his aim not to be hit. To have a lesser aim would be the height of folly for the soldier, and it is just as dangerous for us in the battle with sin.

Is there any place for grace? Most assuredly; in fact, the Apostle Paul based his call for such decisive commitment on God's mercy or grace. (Paul seems to use mercy and grace interchangeably without regard to the precise distinction in their respective meanings.) Let's look again at Romans 12:1, "Therefore, I urge you, brothers, in view of God's mercy, to offer your bodies as living sacrifices, holy and pleasing to God—this is your spiritual act of worship."

It was in view of God's mercy that Paul urged the

Romans, and us today, to commit their bodies as living sacrifices, holy and pleasing to God. Undoubtedly Paul had in mind the mercy of God as he had displayed it in the preceding chapters: the mercy of God in our salvation. He could have been thinking of the righteousness of God that comes to us by faith, of justification freely by His grace through the redemption that is in Christ Jesus, or of God presenting Jesus as a propitiation for our sins that turns aside God's just and holy wrath from us.

No doubt Paul's mind would once again have dwelt on that wonderful statement in Romans 4:8—

"Blessed is the man
whose sin the Lord will never count against him."

He would have thought of the fact that, having been justified through faith, we now have peace with God, and that we now stand before Him in grace every day. He would have rejoiced in our deliverance from the dominion of sin through our union with Christ in His death. He would have once again exulted in that fantastic statement in Romans 8:1 that "there is now no condemnation for those who are in Christ Jesus."

He would have relished again the promises of future glory and of the assurance that even in this life nothing can separate us from the love of God that is in Christ Jesus. He would have reflected again with amazement upon God's mercy to the Gentiles and the promise of future mercy to the Jews. In short, Paul would have had in mind the gospel of Jesus Christ in all its wonderfulness when he wrote of the mercy of God.

It is this mercy that is revealed to us in the gospel and that we believers have experienced that is the ground for our commitment. Such a commitment as Paul called for would indeed be a legalistic and oppressive commitment if it were not grounded in love. And the only way Paul would stir up our love is to remind us of God's love for us, revealed through His mercy and His grace. What Paul asked for from us is only a response of love and gratitude, which expresses itself in loving commitment.

John Calvin commented on Romans 12:1 as follows:

> Paul's entreaty teaches us that men will never worship God with a sincere heart, or be roused to fear and obey Him with sufficient zeal, until they properly understand how much they are indebted to His mercy. . . . Paul, . . . in order to bind us to God not by servile fear but by a voluntary and cheerful love of righteousness, attracts us by the sweetness of that grace in which our salvation consists.[7]

So we see once again the relationship of grace and discipline. A loving response to God's grace and mercy is the only motive acceptable to God for the commitment Paul called for. And it is the continual reminding of ourselves of His grace and mercy that provides the only enduring motivation to sustain such a commitment and keep it from becoming oppressive. That is why we must preach the gospel to ourselves every day.

One further encouragement to commitment is found in the context of Romans 6:13. You remember that Romans 6:13 is a parallel passage to Romans 12:1, in that in both passages Paul called on us to offer our bodies to God in the pursuit of holiness. But the context of Romans 6:13 is the assurance of God's enablement to carry out that commitment. In Romans 6:11 we are urged to count ourselves dead to the dominion of sin and alive to the enabling power of God. In verse 14, Paul assures us that "sin shall not be [our] master, because [we] are not under law, but under grace." In other words, God not only asks us to commit ourselves to the pursuit of holiness, but provides the grace to enable us to do it. As the little verse we saw in chapter 5 says, "He bids us fly and gives us wings."

Grace, of course, as used in this setting refers to God's

divine enablement through the power of His Spirit. So whether it is grace viewed as God's undeserved favor as we would understand it in Romans 12:1, or viewed as God's divine enablement as we should understand it in the context of Romans 6:13, it is grace that is the basis for our commitment to the pursuit of holiness.

So an all-out, unreserved, nothing-held-back commitment to the pursuit of holiness may be exhausting, but it will not be oppressive if it is grounded in grace. But to be grounded in grace, it must be continually referred back to the gospel. So don't just preach the gospel to yourself every day merely to experience the cleansing of your conscience. You certainly need to do so for that reason. But as you do so, reaffirm, as a response of love and gratitude to God, your commitment to Him. And do so in reliance on His Spirit that by His grace He will enable you to carry out your commitment.

And by the way, if you have not already done so, don't neglect to list specific areas of temptation where you want to make a commitment. Take these to the Lord and with a full view of His mercy to you, commit yourself to deal with these areas of your life.

10

THE DISCIPLINE
OF CONVICTIONS

Do not conform any longer to the pattern of this world,
but be transformed by the renewing of your mind.
Then you will be able to test
and approve what God's will is—
his good, pleasing and perfect will.
ROMANS 12:2

IN THE EARLY 1990s the authors of a book on contemporary American society wrote, "In the 1950s and even in the early 1960s, there was something much closer to a moral consensus in America. . . . There is absolutely no moral consensus at all in the 1990s. Everyone is making up their own personal moral code—their own Ten Commandments."[1]

It should not surprise us that society in general has moved in the direction of ancient Israel when "every man did that which was right in his own eyes" (Judges 21:25, KJV). Western civilization has deliberately turned away from the Bible as its moral authority. Now we are suffering the consequences.

What should disturb us, however, is that evangelicals are moving in the same direction. "Four out of 10 people who call themselves evangelicals don't believe there is such a thing as absolute truth, according to a Barna Research Group poll."[2] If this means that these 40 percent decide for themselves what is right and wrong instead of going to the Bible, then it is no wonder there is often little difference between the ethical views and behavior of professing Christians and those who have nothing to do with Christianity. Morality becomes merely a matter of one's personal opinion. In fact, I am aware of situations where Christians were confronted about sin in their lives and responded, "That's just your opinion."

Let's move closer to home, however. What about the remaining 60 percent of evangelicals who apparently do believe there is such a thing as absolute truth? Does such a belief affect our behavior or change our character? To what degree does a belief that the Bible sets forth absolute truth determine the way we live? To a large extent, the answer must be very little, for the simple reason that so many believers are not exposing themselves to the truths of Scripture on a daily basis.

It seems that in many evangelical circles we do have morality by consensus. We may not be doing what is right in our own eyes, as society around us is doing, but neither are we living according to biblical standards. Instead we live according to the standard of conduct of Christians around us. We not only have morality by consensus; we have sanctification by consensus. We expect to become holy by osmosis, by the absorption of the ethical values of our Christian peer group.

If we are going to make progress in the pursuit of holiness, we must aim to live according to the precepts of Scripture—not according to the culture, even Christian culture, around us. But how can we do this if we don't know what those precepts are? It is not sufficient for us to hear one or two thirty-minute sermons a week. We must be exposed to the Scriptures on a daily basis if we hope to live under their authority.

To pursue holiness, one of the disciplines we must become skilled in is the development of *Bible-based convictions*. A conviction is a determinative belief: something you believe so strongly that it affects the way you live. Someone has observed that a belief is what you hold, but a conviction is what holds you. You may live contrary to what you believe, but you cannot live contrary to your convictions. (This doesn't mean you never *act* contrary to your convictions, but that you do not consistently violate them.) So the discipline we are talking about is the development of *convictions*, not mere beliefs. Convictions, of course, can be good or bad, so we want to make sure our convictions are Bible-based, that they are derived from our personal interaction with the Scriptures.

THE INFLUENCE CONTINUUM

In the last chapter we saw that, in Romans 12:1, the Apostle Paul made a strong appeal to us to make a commitment of ourselves to God to live lives holy and pleasing to Him. In the following verse, he began to tell us how to carry this out, and the first thing he said was to develop Bible-based convictions. Here is how he put it:

> Do not conform any longer to the pattern of this world, but be transformed by the renewing of your mind. Then you will be able to test and approve what God's will is—his good, pleasing and perfect will. (Romans 12:2)

As we look at Romans 12:2, one of the first things we see is that Paul established a contrast between conforming (or being conformed) to the pattern of this world and being transformed by the renewal of one's mind. He assumes there are only two alternatives. Our convictions and values will come from society around us (the world), or they will come as our minds are renewed by the Word of God. There is no third option.

The writer of Psalm 1 stated this truth in a similar fashion. He said,

> Blessed is the man
> who does not walk in the counsel of the wicked

> or stand in the way of sinners
>> or sit in the seat of mockers.
> But his delight is in the law of the LORD,
>> and on his law he meditates day and night.
> He is like a tree planted by streams of water,
>> which yields its fruit in season
> and whose leaf does not wither.
>> Whatever he does prospers. (Psalm 1:1-3)

The psalmist envisions two alternatives, or two groups of people. Those described in verse 1 (by way of the negative expression *does not*) are being drawn more and more under the controlling influence of wicked people, until at last they themselves begin to influence others. To "sit in the seat of mockers" probably refers to a position of influence and authority similar to that exercised by the teachers of the law who "sit in Moses' seat" (Matthew 23:2). So these people are not only captive to sin themselves, but influence others to sin.

The second group of people are those who delight in the law of God and meditate on it, or think about it continually. Again note that the psalmist presents a contrast between two diametrically opposing influences: the pervasive influence of sinful society or the life-changing influence of the law of God. There is no neutral sphere of influence. We are being influenced by the forces of sinful society or we are being influenced by the Word of God.

The truth is, of course, that we believers are probably being influenced by both society and the Word of God. We can think of these two opposing influences as representing the two extreme ends of a continuum, as shown in the following illustration:

Sinful	Word
Society	of God

All of us who are believers are somewhere on that continuum, partially influenced by sinful society and partially influenced by the Word of God. The more we are influenced by society, the more we move toward the left end of the continuum. The more we are influenced by the Word of God, the more we move to the right. What determines whether we are moving to the left or to the right? The psalmist gives us the answer: our attitude toward the Word of God and the time we spend thinking about it. *Nothing else will determine where you are on that continuum.*

The person who is living toward the right end of the continuum is described, first of all, as one who delights in the law of God. Like the Apostle Paul, this person has determined that God's law is "holy, righteous and good" (Romans 7:12). He or she sees that God's law is not onerous or burdensome, but is given to help us please God and live lives that are productive and satisfying (see Psalm 1:3). One who delights in the law of God sees the Bible not just as a book of rules that are difficult to live by, but as the Word of his or her heavenly Father who is the God of all grace and deals with him or her in grace.

The person living toward the right end of the continuum also meditates on God's law day and night. As used in Scripture, the word *meditate* means to think about a truth with a view to its meaning and application to one's life. As God told Joshua, "Meditate on [the Book of the Law] day and night, so that you may be careful to do everything written in it" (Joshua 1:8). It is the application, or the "doing," that should be the goal of meditation. Included in this concept of meditation is reflection on one's own life to determine what conformity, or lack of it, there is between the scriptural truth and one's character or conduct. As the psalmist said,

> I have considered my ways
> and have turned my steps to your statutes.
> (Psalm 119:59)

He not only thought about Scripture. He also thought about his life and the extent to which it conformed to Scripture.

"Day and night" is an expression for *continually*. If we want to live toward the right end of the continuum of influence, our minds must be steeped in the Scriptures. We must constantly turn our minds to the Word of God, pondering the meaning and application of its truths to our lives. The idea of continual meditation may seem unrealistic and unattainable in our busy age when our minds need to be occupied with the various responsibilities we all have. "How can I meditate on Scripture," you may ask, "when I have to think about my work all day long?"

We should not think of the concept of "continually" as meaning every moment. Rather we should think in terms of consistently and habitually. What does your mind turn to when it is free to turn to anything? Do you begin to meditate on Scripture? I often ask people this question: "When you can think about anything you want to think about, what do you think about?" Do you think about your problems, or do you engage in mental arguing with someone else, or perhaps even allow your mind to drift into the wasteland of impure thoughts? Thinking is our most constant activity. Our thoughts are our constant occupation. We are never without them. But we can choose the direction and content of those thoughts.

Meditation on Scripture is a *discipline*. We must commit ourselves to be proactive. We must memorize key passages (or carry them on cards) so that we can think about them. We must be alert for those times during the day when we can turn our minds to the Word of God, and then we must *do* it. Even the practice of daily Bible reading is insufficient if we go the rest of the day without meditating on some truths of Scripture. We must choose to meditate instead of thinking about other things, or listening to the radio, or watching television. We simply have to decide which end of the influence continuum we want to live on and take steps accordingly.

One thing we can be sure of: If we do not *actively* seek to come under the influence of God's Word, we *will* come under the influence of sinful society around us. The impact of our culture with its heavy emphasis on materialism, living for one's self, and instant gratification is simply too strong and pervasive for us to not be influenced by it. Once again, there is no such thing as a neutral stance on the continuum of influence. We are being drawn more and more under the transforming influence of Scripture, or we are being progressively drawn into the web of an ungodly society around us.

BE TRANSFORMED
The next thought we see in Romans 12:2 is that we are to be *transformed* by the renewing of our minds. We have already looked at the word *transformed* in chapter 6 when we studied 2 Corinthians 3:18. We saw that it denotes a deep internal change in our character that produces outward change in our behavior. Jesus said that it is "from within, out of men's hearts," that evil thoughts and actions come (Mark 7:21). The transformation that Paul was writing about occurs in the heart and changes it so it does not continue to produce such evil.

We also saw that the verb *being transformed* in 2 Corinthians 3:18 is passive, indicating something that is done to us, in that instance by the Holy Spirit. We noted that the Holy Spirit is the transforming or sanctifying agent. We do not transform ourselves, although we do have a part to play in the process.

The verb *be transformed* in Romans 12:2 is also in the passive voice. Yet it is also an imperative—a command, or in this case, an exhortation. The use of the imperative mood with a passive verb is not common in the English language. When we give a command, or urge someone to do something, we usually use an active verb. The father of a Little League baseball player will call out to his son, "Tommy, hit the ball." He wants Tommy to do something, not have something done to him.

Yet Paul exhorts us to "be transformed." He does not urge us to do something, but to have something done to us.

Another illustration with Tommy, the Little Leaguer, may help us understand what Paul was saying to us. Suppose Tommy comes in from his game all grimy with sweat and dirty from sliding into second base. His mother is preparing for guests for dinner that evening. She takes one look at Tommy and says to him, "Go take a shower."

That's a command. It is an imperative and she uses an active verb. She wants Tommy to do something. But what is the end result Tommy's mother wants? She wants Tommy to be made clean, so she directs him to take a shower. She knows Tommy cannot cleanse himself. If he tried, all he would do is rearrange the dirt. So she wants Tommy to bring himself under the cleansing action of the soap and water. It is the soap and water that will wash away the sweat and the dirt, but Tommy must bring himself under their cleansing action. So his mother says to him, "Go take a shower."

Just as Tommy cannot cleanse himself, so we cannot transform ourselves. Only the Holy Spirit can do that. But just as Tommy must bring himself under the cleansing action of the soap and water, so we must bring ourselves under the transforming action of the Holy Spirit. This means, of course, that we must continually submit our minds to the Word of God, which is the chief instrument the Holy Spirit uses to transform us.

So when Paul urged us to "be transformed by the renewing of your mind," he was essentially saying, "Bring yourself under the transforming influence of the Word of God." It is by this means that we begin to develop Bible-based convictions.

Paul's exhortation to be transformed is also in the present tense. This means we are to continue to let ourselves be transformed. It is a continuous process that should be occurring every day of our lives. As John Murray said, "We are to be constantly in the process of being metamorphosed by renewal of that which is the seat of thought and understanding."[3] It is more than just our thoughts and understanding that need to be changed. We must also be changed in our affections and wills. But it begins with our understanding the truth. Nineteenth-century Scottish commentator John Brown wrote,

> The mind is renewed when, under the influence of the Spirit, the truth is understood and believed, so as to displace the ignorance and error that previously prevailed. It is the truth, understood and believed, that purifies the heart from the love of the world; and, just in proportion as that truth is understood and believed, are men transformed. It is by men's being formed to a right way of thinking, that they are formed to a right way of feeling and acting with regard to this world and the next—to God, and our brethren of mankind.[4]

SEARCH THE SCRIPTURES

Of course, we need to be sure that, in thinking about Scripture and its application to our lives, we are thinking God's truth, not our own opinions. This means, first of all, that we must be absolutely convinced that the Bible is God's Word—that what Scripture says, God says. We need to approach the Bible with the deep, settled conviction that it accurately expresses the mind of God and the will of God as to how we are to live.

Ambivalence on this point can be fatal to the pursuit of holiness, for after all, only God is the final authority on what constitutes holy living. If the Bible is not the complete, authoritative Word of God, then there is no absolute moral truth, and we are left to our own opinions.

The Bible, however, consistently affirms that it is indeed the very Word of God. The Apostle Paul said, "All Scripture is God-breathed" (2 Timothy 3:16). The Apostle Peter said that "men spoke from God as they were carried along by the Holy Spirit" (2 Peter 1:21). Expressions such as, "the Holy Spirit spoke . . . through the mouth of David" (Acts 1:16) or Moses or one of the prophets occur frequently in the New

Testament. Peter spoke of Paul's writings as Scripture (2 Peter 3:16).

We may not understand how the Holy Spirit moved upon the minds of those who wrote the Scriptures, or how He spoke through the mouths of such men as David so that what they wrote or said was exactly what He wanted them to say, but this is what the Bible consistently affirms. If this is a new thought to you, or if you have some doubts about this, I urge you to make this issue a matter of prayerful, humble study. Ask God to remove any doubts you might have and give you a settled conviction that the Bible is indeed God's Word, that it is complete and authoritative, and that it is absolute truth.

It is not enough, however, to believe that all Scripture is from God. We need to strive to understand it as best we possibly can. We need to approach the Bible each day with a spirit of deep humility, recognizing that our understanding of spiritual truth is at best incomplete and to some extent inaccurate. No Christian or body of Christians has a corner on all of truth. At one time Jesus said, "I praise you, Father, Lord of heaven and earth, because you have hidden these things from the wise and learned, and revealed them to little children. Yes, Father, for this was your good pleasure" (Luke 10:21).

However knowledgeable about Scripture we may be, we need to approach it each day as little children, asking the Holy Spirit to teach us. Regardless of how much we already know and understand, there is still an infinite storehouse of understanding of the mind of God waiting for us in Scripture. My own experience, based on more than forty years of studying the Bible, is that the more I learn and understand of Scripture, the more I see how little I do understand of all that God has revealed to us in His Word. So as you approach the reading or study of the Bible, don't do so just to buttress you own previously held opinions or to affirm your favorite doctrines. Rather, ask the Holy Spirit to teach you.

Pray as the psalmist did that God will open your eyes to see wonderful things in His law, and that He will give you understanding so as to keep His law (Psalm 119:18,34). He may indeed affirm your doctrines and confirm your convictions more deeply as you see them aligned with the teaching of Scripture. He will also very likely make you aware of areas of your life where you are not fully obedient to His revealed will, or He may cause you to see that another group of believers who hold a different doctrinal position from yours do have Scriptures that they believe support their views. So we should approach the Scriptures in humility and expect the Holy Spirit to humble us even further as we continue to be taught by Him from His Word.

Next, we need to approach the Scriptures with an attitude of mental discipline. We have already seen in chapter 8 that we need both discipline and dependence in the pursuit of holiness. The same is true in our study of the Scriptures. There are many approaches to and methods of Bible study, but common to all of them is an attitude of dependent diligence. This attitude is well expressed by Solomon in Proverbs 2:1-5—

> My son, if you accept my words
> and store up my commands within you,
> turning your ear to wisdom
> and applying your heart to understanding,
> and if you call out for insight
> and cry aloud for understanding,
> and if you look for it as for silver
> and search for it as for hidden treasure,
> then you will understand the fear of the LORD
> and find the knowledge of God.

Here again we see that there must be a spirit of humility as expressed by the phrase "if you accept my words" (verse 1). This attitude is contrasted with the attitude of the foolish—

> since they would not accept my advice
> and spurned my rebuke. (Proverbs 1:30)

The practice of diligent study is expressed by the phrases "applying your heart to understanding," "if you look for it as for silver," and "[if you] search for it as for hidden treasure." The thought of searching the Scriptures with the same intensity that one would search for hidden treasures suggests the value that we should put on the teaching of Scripture. Solomon also spoke of this value when he said, "Guard my teachings as the apple of your eye" (Proverbs 7:2).

The question we must ask ourselves is this: What value do we place upon the Word of God? Do we search it as if we were seeking for hidden treasures, or do we read it and study it only because we know it is something we should do?

Along with an attitude of diligence, we also need an attitude of dependence such as is expressed in verse 3:

> And if you call out for insight
> and cry aloud for understanding.

"Calling out" and "crying aloud" denote an almost desperate sense of dependence; an attitude far different from a more usual perfunctory prayer for God to teach us as we begin our weekly Bible study. The question is, do we really believe we are dependent upon the Holy Spirit to enlighten our understanding, or do we actually depend on our own intellectual ability in our study of Scripture? I suspect that many of us, while giving lip service to dependence on the Spirit, actually depend on our own intellect.

It is difficult to maintain an attitude of both diligence and dependence, but we must do this if we want to learn from the Holy Spirit. He does not reward either indolence or sinful self-confidence. He does bless diligence when it is pursued in a sincere attitude of dependence on Him. What we are talking about here is not just acquiring more knowledge of biblical truth, but rather the development of Bible-based convictions by which we are to live.

We can acquire increased knowledge of scriptural truth in the same way we can increase our knowledge of science or history. Unfortunately, too many Christians seem to approach Bible study in the same way they would approach those more academic subjects. When we do this we are more apt to become proud rather than humble. We become proud over our "superior" knowledge of biblical truth rather than humbled over our lack of obedience to what Scripture teaches. Again, we need to pray with the psalmist,

> Teach me, O LORD, to follow your decrees;
> then I will keep them to the end.
> (Psalm 119:33)

That is, we should pray for knowledge of truth that will change our lives rather than simply inform our minds.

STORE IT UP

We see then that before we can successfully meditate on Scripture, we need to have an accurate understanding of what it says—not just intellectually but in our hearts. We need to know what God says to us about how we should live. This demands humble, dependent, disciplined Bible study. It also requires that we "store up" God's truth in our minds and hearts.

Solomon used the expression "store up my commands within you" in Proverbs 2:1 and 7:1. The idea behind "store up" is to lay away in anticipation of a future need. When I was a boy my mother canned a lot of fruits and vegetables during the summer when they were plentiful. In doing that she was storing up food in anticipation of the months ahead when those fruits and vegetables would not be available in her garden.

A well-known verse of Scripture is Psalm 119:11, which says,

> I have hidden your word in my heart
> that I might not sin against you.

The word *hidden* in that Scripture does not mean hidden in the sense that something is deliberately put out of sight to conceal its location. Rather, it means to store up, or more accurately, to treasure up. So it also suggests the same sense of storing up as do Proverbs 2:1 and 7:1, but with the added dimension that what is stored up is of great value and is to be treasured.

This is the way we should regard and treat the Word of God. Looking back again at Proverbs 2:1-5, we see that, immediately following the strong exhortation to dependent, diligent study, is the assertion in verse 6 that the Lord gives wisdom, knowledge, and understanding. In the context it is obvious that He gives these in response to our searching the Scriptures in the way described in verses 1-4.

Then in Proverbs 3:13-15 we read this assessment of the wisdom and understanding God gives to those who search His Word in His way:

> Blessed is the man who finds wisdom,
>   the man who gains understanding,
> for she is more profitable than silver
>   and yields better returns than gold.
> She is more precious than rubies;
>   nothing you desire can compare with her.

The wisdom and understanding that Solomon described is what we might call "spiritual" wisdom and understanding as opposed to mere human wisdom. Basically Solomon is referring to principles of life that, if followed, will enable us to live lives pleasing to God. The Apostle Paul referred to this kind of wisdom when he wrote to the Colossian believers that he was praying for them, "asking God to fill you with the knowledge of his will through all spiritual wisdom and understanding. And we pray this in order that you may live a life worthy of the Lord and may please him in every way" (Colossians 1:9-10).

Note, however, the tremendously high value Solomon placed on spiritual wisdom. It is more profitable than silver, yields better returns than gold, and is more precious than rubies. In fact, he said *nothing* can compare with it. We can now see why the psalmist spoke of treasuring up God's Word in his heart.

How then do we treasure up God's Word in our hearts? The answer is through continual meditation on Scripture. In order to think about Scripture continually, however, we need to have it in our minds. The best way to do this is through the discipline of memorizing key passages of Scripture. I am very much aware that Scripture memorization has largely fallen by the wayside in our day of microwave meals and television entertainment. But let me say as graciously but as firmly as I can: We cannot effectively pursue holiness without the Word of God stored up in our minds where it can be used by the Holy Spirit to transform us.

Remember, we are to be transformed by the renewing of our minds. We have already seen that each of us lives on a continuum of influence between society around us and the Word of God. There simply is no better way to move toward the "Word of God" end of the continuum than through the discipline of Scripture memorization. I know it requires work and is sometimes discouraging when we can't recall accurately a verse we have worked hard to memorize. The truth is, however, *all* forms of discipline require work and are often discouraging. But the person who perseveres in any discipline, despite the hard work and discouraging times, reaps the reward the discipline is intended to produce.[5]

The example of Jesus' use of Scripture when He was tempted by the Devil in the wilderness is often used as a challenge to us to memorize Scripture. Three times He was tempted, and three times He answered Satan's temptation by resorting to the Scriptures saying, "It is written" (Matthew 4:1-11). It is obvious He had memorized these Old Testament commands that He effectively used to thwart Satan's assaults. But it should also be apparent to us that Jesus knew more than a few isolated verses of the Mosaic Law. Rather, His mind was steeped in the Scriptures. If you and I are going to be holy as He is holy, our minds must also be filled with Scripture. In the words of Paul, we must "let the word of Christ dwell in [us] richly" (Colossians 3:16).

Christ's use of specific Scriptures to thwart Satan's temptations should, however, be instructive to us. I have already referred to identifying specific temptations to which you are vulnerable and listing them on a private prayer page. Then in the last chapter I urged you to make specific commitments regarding the same areas of vulnerability. In Christ's example we see this specificity taken one step further as He brought particular passages from the Old Testament to bear on the temptations He faced. So I encourage you to memorize Scriptures that deal with the particular temptations to which you are especially vulnerable. Then ask the Holy Spirit to bring them to your mind at times of temptation.

APPLY TO YOUR LIFE

We have seen that bringing ourselves under the transforming influence of the Word of God means much more than just acquiring knowledge about the contents of Scripture. In fact, the mere acquisition of Bible facts or doctrinal truth without application to one's life can lead to spiritual pride. As Paul said, "Knowledge puffs up, but love builds up" (1 Corinthians 8:1). By contrast Paul also spoke of "the knowledge of the truth that leads to godliness" (Titus 1:1).

What is the difference between these two concepts of Bible knowledge? In the first instance the Corinthians were using their knowledge in a selfish and prideful way. They were "looking down their noses" at people with different convictions from theirs. On the other hand, the knowledge that leads to godliness is knowledge of the Scriptures that is being applied to one's life and results in godly behavior.

One of the banes of present-day evangelical Christianity is the way we sit every week under the teaching of God's Word, or even have private devotions and perhaps participate in a Bible study group, without a serious intent to obey the truth we learn. The indictment of the Jewish people God made to Ezekiel could well be said of us today:

"My people come to you, as they usually do, and sit before you to listen to your words, but they do not put them into practice. . . . Indeed, to them you are nothing more than one who sings love songs with a beautiful voice and plays an instrument well, for they hear your words but do not put them into practice." (Ezekiel 33:31-32)

Our tendency seems to be to equate knowledge of the truth, and even agreement with it, with obedience to it. James said when we do this we deceive ourselves (James 1:22). This is especially true when we focus on the more scandalous sins "out there" in society to the neglect of the more "refined" sins we commit.

We can not develop Bible-based convictions merely by storing up Bible knowledge in our heads. We do not even develop them by personal Bible study and Scripture memorization, though those practices certainly help us get started. As we begin to meditate on Scripture consistently we come closer. But convictions are really developed when we begin to apply the teachings of Scripture to real-life situations.

My wife and I recently went shopping for a coffee table. We had agreed on the style we wanted and very quickly found one at a price within our range. I am the type of person who is ready to buy as soon as I find what I like, but my wife is a "shopper." She likes to look at everything in the store. Sure enough, she soon came upon her "dream" coffee table, a rather uncommon design that she had dreamed about for years but never thought she would own. But as you might guess—and as is always the case—it was more expensive.

I started talking about being good stewards of the money God has given us, but God started "talking" to me (through the convicting work of His Spirit) about husbands loving their wives, just as Christ loved the Church (Ephesians 5:25). As I worked through that situation, I realized one of the concrete ways I was to love my wife was to be more sensitive to her dreams and desires. In that situation God was desirous that I learn more about what it means for husbands to love their wives than that I be a good steward of His resources. But the point of my story is this: I knew Ephesians 5:25. I believed it, had memorized it, and meditated on it. But through the application of it in a real-life situation, I deepened my conviction about it. I have found since that incident that I am more sensitive to what it means in a practical way for me to love my wife as Christ loved the Church in a sacrificial self-giving way.

So it is through knowledge, plus meditation, plus application of the Scriptures to concrete situations in our daily lives that we develop Bible-based convictions. And, as we develop those convictions, we will be transformed by the Holy Spirit more and more into the likeness of Christ.

ANY ROOM FOR GRACE?

We have looked at some difficult disciplines in this chapter: diligent but dependent Bible study, Scripture memorization, continual meditation, and application of Scripture to real-life situations. Actually, these disciplines are not all that difficult, but they can certainly appear that way to those who have never before practiced them. So the question may arise in some minds, Is there any room for grace in the practice of the disciplines necessary to develop Bible-based convictions? What happens if I stumble along in Scripture memorization, for example?

What does happen if we stumble or fall in the practice of these disciplines? First of all, God does not love us any less. His love for us is based solely on the fact that we are in union with His Son Jesus Christ. That is what the gospel is all about. Christ's righteousness has become our righteousness. Our sins were laid upon Him, and the penalty for them was fully paid by Him on the cross. Daily His blood cleanses us from all sin. God's grace, His unmerited favor, is never conditioned on our performance, but always on the unchanging merit of our Lord Jesus Christ.

Our progress in the pursuit of holiness, however, *is* conditioned on our practice of the disciplines God has given us. It is true that we are transformed more and more into the likeness of Christ by the Holy Spirit. It is also true, however, that one of the chief means—in fact, probably *the* chief means—He uses is the renewing of our minds. And the Apostle Paul was quite emphatic in Romans 12:2 about our submitting ourselves to the transforming influence of the Word of God by which our minds are renewed.

Therefore, we may say that our *acceptance* by God the Father is based solely on His grace to us through Christ. His favor is never earned by what we do nor forfeited by what we don't do. But we may say with equal emphasis that our progress in the pursuit of holiness is to a significant degree conditioned on our use of the disciplines that God has appointed for us. And they have been appointed by God. They have not been initiated by the "disciplined" school of discipleship. They were initiated by God.

Everything I have said about the disciplines of Bible study, Scripture memorization, continual meditation, and application of Scripture in daily life has been based on Scripture. I have not developed any manmade theories about Christian growth. All I have done is point out what the Scriptures say about these disciplines. And, as I observed earlier in this chapter, what Scripture says, God says. If we ignore these disciplines, we are ignoring God.

We must always remember, though, that the practice of these disciplines does not earn us any favor with God. It is helpful to distinguish between a *meritorious* cause of God's blessing and an *instrumental* cause. The meritorious cause is always the merit of Christ. We can never add to what He has already done to procure God's blessing on our lives. The instrumental cause, however, is the means or avenues God has ordained to use. God has clearly set forth certain disciplines for us to practice in the pursuit of holiness. As we practice them God will use them in our lives, not because we have earned His blessing, but because we have followed His ordained path of blessing.

We also need to keep in mind that the imperative in Romans 12:2 to be transformed immediately follows the imperative of verse 1, to offer our bodies as living sacrifices, holy and pleasing to Him. The second exhortation, like the first, is based on the mercy of God. The discipline of developing Bible-based convictions, then, should be a response to the mercy and grace of God to us through Christ. If we truly desire to live by grace, then we will want to respond to that grace by seeking to live lives that are pleasing to God. And we simply cannot do that if we do not practice the disciplines necessary to develop Bible-based convictions.

11

THE DISCIPLINE OF CHOICES

*Just as you used to offer the parts of your body
in slavery to impurity and to ever-increasing wickedness,
so now offer them in slavery to righteousness
leading to holiness.*
ROMANS 6:19

A DEFINING MOMENT in my life occurred very quietly one evening in the first Bible study group I attended. The leader of the study said to us, "The Bible was not given just to increase your knowledge but to guide your conduct." As obvious as that truth is to me now, at the time it was a brand-new thought. It was literally as if someone had turned on a light in my mind. I saw clearly what I had been completely oblivious to before.

It wasn't that I was living what we would consider a sinful lifestyle. In fact, quite the opposite was true. I had grown up in a church setting, had trusted Christ as my Savior, had read the Bible every day, and had even memorized a few Bible verses. But the idea of applying Scripture to specific situations in my daily life had never occurred to me. That night I prayed a simple prayer, "God, starting tonight I want You to use the Bible to guide my conduct." My whole approach to the Word of God changed overnight, and the Scriptures suddenly became very relevant to my daily life.

That was the beginning of my own personal "pursuit of holiness."

The Bible is indeed a very relevant book giving instruction and guidance for our daily lives. In following this instruction, however, we are continually faced with a series of choices. Of course, life is a constant series of choices from the time we arise in the morning until we go to bed at night. Many of these choices have moral consequences. For example, the route you choose to drive to your work each morning is probably not morally significant, but the thoughts you choose to think while you are driving and the way you choose to drive are moral choices.

ONE CHOICE AT A TIME

We have looked at Ephesians 4:25-32 in chapter 5 as illustrative of the putting-off–putting-on principle. Now let's look at it in the light of choices we must make. For your convenience I will reproduce that passage of Scripture:

> Therefore each of you must put off falsehood and speak truthfully to his neighbor, for we are all members of one body. "In your anger do not sin": Do not let the sun go down while you are still angry, and do not give the devil a foothold. He who has been stealing must steal no longer, but must work, doing something useful with his own hands, that he may have something to share with those in need.
>
> Do not let any unwholesome talk come out of your mouths, but only what is helpful for building others up according to their needs, that it may benefit those who listen. And do not grieve the Holy Spirit of God, with whom you were sealed for the day of redemption. Get rid of all bitterness, rage and anger, brawling and slander, along with every form of malice. Be kind and compassionate to one another, forgiving each other, just as in Christ God forgave you.

As we go down the list of practical instructions the Apostle Paul gave us, we see that we can choose to:

❖ Tell the truth or tell a lie.
❖ Deal with anger or let it smolder.
❖ Be absolutely honest in our finances or effectively steal (from the government or our employer, for example).
❖ Share with others in need or spend our resources on ourselves.
❖ Speak only what is helpful to others or speak unwholesome words (criticism, gossip, complaining, etc.)
❖ Be kind, compassionate, and forgiving or harbor bitterness, anger, and resentment.

In other words, the practice of putting off sinful attitudes and actions and putting on Christlike character involves a constant series of choices. We choose in every situation which direction we will go. It is through these choices that we develop Christlike habits of living. Habits are developed by repetition, and it is in the arena of moral choices that we develop spiritual habit patterns.

We see this development of moral habits in one direction or the other in Romans 6:19, "Just as you used to offer the parts of your body in slavery to impurity and to ever-increasing wickedness, so now offer them in slavery to righteousness leading to holiness." The believers at Rome had formerly offered the parts of their bodies to impurity and to *ever-increasing* wickedness. The more they sinned, the more they were inclined to sin. They were continually deepening their habit patterns of sin simply through their practice of making sinful choices.

What was true of the Romans can be just as true of us today. Sin tends to cloud our reason, dull our consciences, stimulate our sinful desires, and weaken our wills. Because of this, each sin we commit reinforces the habit of sinning and makes it easier to give in to that temptation the next time we encounter it.

Paul wanted the Roman believers, and us today, to turn in the other direction and to develop habits of godly living. He said, "So now offer [the parts of your body] in slavery to righteousness leading to holiness." Righteousness, in this passage, does not refer to the righteousness we have in Christ (as in Romans 3), but to the ethical righteousness—the right conduct—we are to practice every day. Whereas righteousness in this verse refers to our conduct, holiness refers to our character. *So it is through righteous actions that we develop holy character.* Holiness of character, then, is developed one choice at a time as we choose to act righteously in each and every situation and circumstance we encounter during the day.

All that we have studied in the last few chapters has been leading us to this point. We do not become more holy either by discipline or by dependence. Neither do we become more holy by committing ourselves to God, or by developing Bible-based convictions. We become more holy by obedience to the Word of God, by choosing to obey His will as revealed in the Scriptures in all the various circumstances of our lives.

It is just as true, however, that the discipline and dependence, the commitment and convictions are absolutely necessary to our making the right choices. We do not make our choices in a vacuum. They are determined by the convictions we have developed and the conscious or unconscious commitments we have made. And it is certainly true that, given the remaining presence of indwelling sin, we can make the right choices only through the enabling power of the Holy Spirit. But all of these principles and means of spiritual growth find their ultimate fulfillment only when we obey God's commandments one choice at a time. And as we obey one choice at a time, our righteous actions lead to holy character.

While I have been writing this book, my wife has begun

to make a quilt. As I have observed her work, I have learned that she first makes a number of quilt "squares," each one foot square. It is the design she sews into each of those squares that determines the overall pattern of the quilt. The particular design she has chosen, a mariner's compass, is rather intricate, with each square containing about forty rather narrow triangles. Each quilt square is beautiful and is a testimony to her sewing ability. But those individual squares, as beautiful as they are, do not make a quilt. It is only when they are sewn together with a narrow strip of cloth between each row of squares that they become a quilt.

The pursuit of holiness may be likened to a quilt. We have the quilt square of discipline, the square of dependence, of commitment, of convictions, and of beholding the glory of Christ in the gospel. Each one of these "squares" is beautiful in and of itself. But if we just look at these principles and means of holiness individually, we still do not have the "quilt" of holiness. What joins all these principles and means together to form the "quilt of holiness" is obedience. And we obey one choice at a time.

TRAIN YOURSELF IN THE RIGHT DIRECTION
In an earlier chapter we looked briefly at 1 Timothy 4:7, where Paul exhorted Timothy to "train yourself to be godly." We saw that in the word *train* Paul used a word from the athletic arena, a word used to describe the training activity of young men as they prepared themselves to compete in the athletic games of that day. Just as those young men trained themselves physically in order to compete in the games, so Paul wanted Timothy, and now us, to train ourselves spiritually toward godliness. Though godliness is a broader concept than holiness (see my discussion of godliness and ungodliness in chapter 5, page 83), holiness is a major part of it, so training ourselves to be godly certainly includes training ourselves in holiness.

The important point, however, is that we train ourselves through exercise. In fact, the *King James Version* translates this phrase as, "exercise thyself rather unto godliness." And how do we exercise ourselves in the spiritual realm? Through the choices we make.

What happens when we make wrong choices, when we choose to sin instead of obey God's Word? We train ourselves in the wrong direction. We reinforce the sinful habits we have already developed and allow them to gain greater strength in our souls.

Consider 2 Peter 2:14—"With eyes full of adultery, they never stop sinning; they seduce the unstable; they are experts in greed—an accursed brood!" This is part of the Apostle Peter's description and scathing denunciation of false teachers, and in verse 14 we are right in the middle of it. The key phrase in verse 14 for our present purpose is, "they are experts in greed." The *New American Standard* Bible says they have a "heart trained in greed." The word *trained* is the same verb Paul used when he wrote, "train yourself to be godly." Peter said the false teachers had *trained* themselves to be greedy. They had trained themselves to the point where, in the very colorful but accurate expression of the *New International Version*, they had become "experts in greed."

All of us have watched the Olympic Games on television. After each event, the three top competitors stand on a platform while a representative of the Olympic committee hangs around each of their necks a ribbon with a gold, silver, or bronze medal on it. They are the "experts" in that particular event. Peter's description of the false teachers reminds me of that aspect of the Olympic Games. It is as if he has hung around the necks of each of these false teachers a ribbon with a medal that says "Expert in Greed."

How had these teachers become experts in greed? For one thing they had obviously committed themselves to the pursuit of financial gain through their false teaching. Beyond that commitment, however, they had made a continuous series of choices to teach false doctrine that would line their pockets. (Verse 3 says, "In their greed these teachers will exploit you with the stories they have made up.") They had pursued those choices so long that they had become experts in greed. They had trained themselves in greed one choice at a time.

These false teachers had become experts, but in the wrong direction. Instead of becoming experts in generosity and self-giving sacrifice, they had become experts in greed. Instead of training themselves to be godly, they had trained themselves to be greedy. The word translated as "train" in the *New International Version* can just as accurately be translated as "discipline," and is in fact translated that way in the *New American Standard* Bible in 1 Timothy 4:7. So these false teachers were disciplined, but in the wrong direction.

The message implied in 2 Peter 2:14 is very sobering. It is possible to discipline ourselves in the wrong direction. We usually think of disciplined people as those who "have their act together" and do the things they should do when they should be done. But the truth is, we are all disciplined to some degree. *The question is, In which direction are we disciplined?* Every day in some areas of life, we are disciplining ourselves in one direction or the other by the choices we make.

WHERE THE GOING GETS TOUGH

God wants us to train ourselves in the right direction. He wants us to make the right choices. Frankly, this is where the going gets tough. We will agree with the teaching of Scripture about some particular sin, and even make a commitment of sorts to put it out of our lives. But then the temptation to indulge that sin comes once again, and we are unwilling to say no. We are unwilling to make those tough choices. We would like to be rid of that sin, and even pray to God to take it away, but are we willing to say *no* to it?

Remember, every day we are training ourselves in one direction or the other. Every day we are training ourselves toward:

lying	or	truthfulness
selfishness	or	unselfishness
anger	or	forgiveness
impurity	or	purity
irritability	or	patience
covetousness	or	generosity
pride	or	humility
materialism	or	simplicity

Think of the persistent sin patterns in your life that you have already identified and hopefully have made specific commitments about, are praying daily over, and perhaps have even memorized some Scripture verses to help you in your struggle against. We need to be especially vigilant in these areas to make the right choices. We have already made too many wrong choices; that is why these sin patterns are so deeply entrenched in us. It is only through making the right choice to obey God's Word that we will break the habits of sin and develop habits of holiness. This is where we desperately need the power of the Holy Spirit to enable us to make the right choices. So cry out to God every day for His help for that day, and then cry out again each time you are confronted with the choice to sin or to obey.

Dawson Trotman, founder of The Navigators, used to say, "You are going to be what you are now becoming." And what you are now becoming is dependent on the choices you make. So commit yourself to making the right choices, and then look to the Holy Spirit to work in you "to will and to act" (Philippians 2:13) in carrying out that commitment.

THE DISCIPLINE OF MORTIFICATION

Making the right choices to obey God rather than the desires of our sinful natures (or flesh) necessarily involves the discipline of mortification.[1] Mortification? What is that? We don't use that word much anymore. People used to say, "I was mortified," when they meant they were deeply embarrassed or humiliated. To mortify, however, actually means to put to death. I suppose the word *mortician* comes from that root meaning, although morticians don't put people to death. They simply prepare for burial the bodies of people who have already died.

What then does mortification have to do with holiness? Why is it involved in making the right choices? The Apostle Paul gave us the answer in Romans 8:13—"For if you live according to the sinful nature, you will die; but if by the Spirit you put to death [mortify] the misdeeds of the body, you will live."

We see, then, that to make the right choices it is necessary to mortify, or put to death, the misdeeds of the body. The misdeeds of the body are the sinful actions we commit in thought, word, or deed. Paul was more explicit about these misdeeds in Colossians 3:5—"Put to death, therefore, whatever belongs to your earthly nature: sexual immorality, impurity, lust, evil desires and greed, which is idolatry." This list of sinful deeds is not meant to be complete but is only typical of the expressions of sin Paul had in mind when he said to put them to death.

As we look at Romans 8:13, one thing we clearly see is that mortification, or putting sin to death, is our responsibility. Paul said, "*You* put to death." This is something we must do. It is not something we turn over to God. Rather, it is our responsibility, as Paul also emphasized in Colossians 3:5.

We should also note that Paul said, "For if you live according to the sinful nature, you will die." Paul was talking about spiritual, not physical death. The opposite is also true. If we live according to the Spirit—that is, if by Him we "put to death the misdeeds of the body"—we shall live in the spiritual sense. Once again, as he did so frequently, Paul stressed the inextricable link between justification and sanctification. Paul clearly taught that we are saved by grace through faith (Ephesians 2:8), but he also stressed that we are to work out our salvation with fear and trembling (Philippians 2:12); that is, without presuming on the grace of God.

Romans 8:13 is another of those sobering passages that calls for healthy but honest self-examination. Does our pursuit of holiness evidence that we have been saved by grace? This question does not suggest we will ever reach the place where we do not have to contend against the flesh. It does mean that the life of a Christian should be characterized by an earnest desire and sincere effort to put to death the sins of the body.

Although mortification is our responsibility, it can only be done through the enabling power of the Holy Spirit. Paul said, "But if *by the Spirit* you put to death the misdeeds of the body, you will live" (emphasis added). John Owen wrote, "All other ways of discipline are in vain. All other helps leave us helpless. Mortification is only accomplished 'through the Spirit.' . . . by Him alone is it wrought. No other power can accomplish it."[2]

We have already studied the relationship between human discipline and dependence on the Holy Spirit in chapter 8. We saw that the Scriptures emphasize both, but that we tend to emphasize one to the neglect of the other. To some, it seems more spiritual to "just turn it all over to God" and trust Him to do the mortifying. Any mention of our responsibility is dismissed as being only "a work of the flesh."

To other people who stress discipline, it seems more responsible to "just do it." But mortification attempted only by human willpower always ends in self-righteousness or frustration. The more naturally disciplined person tends toward self-righteousness and wonders why everyone else can't be as successful in mortification as he or she is. But all that person has done is exchanged one sin for another. The problem of impure thoughts, for example, is exchanged for pride and self-righteousness. Another person who tries to mortify some particular sin by his or her own willpower fails and becomes frustrated and guilty. So pride or frustration is always the result of attempts to mortify sin that are carried on apart from utter dependence on the Spirit.

HOW TO PUT SIN TO DEATH

What then does it mean to mortify or put to death the misdeeds, that is, the sinful expressions, of the body? First of all, Paul did not say to mortify indwelling sin, but rather *sins*, which are the various expressions of indwelling sin. We cannot eliminate indwelling sin in this life. It will be with us until the day we die.

To mortify a sin means to *subdue* it, to *deprive it of its power*, to break the habit pattern we have developed of continually giving in to the temptation to that particular sin. The *goal* of mortification is *to weaken the habits of sin* so that we do make the right choices.

Mortification involves dealing with all known sin in one's life. Without a purpose to obey all of God's Word, isolated attempts to mortify a particular sin are of no avail. An attitude of *universal* obedience in every area of life is essential. As Paul wrote to the Corinthians, "Let us purify ourselves from *everything* that contaminates body and spirit" (2 Corinthians 7:1, emphasis added). We cannot, for example, mortify impure hearts if we are unwilling to also put to death resentment. We cannot mortify a fiery temper if we are not also seeking to put to death the pride that so often underlies it. Hating one particular sin is not enough. We must hate all sin for what it really is: an expression of rebellion against God.

A man came to me wanting help in dealing with sexual lust in his thoughts and habits. I knew, however, that he had a greater problem in interpersonal relationships. He was critical and judgmental and very vocal about it. His lust bothered him because it made him feel guilty and defeated. His judgmental spirit and critical words didn't bother him, so he was making no effort to deal with those sins. He needed to learn to mortify all sin, not just what made him feel bad about himself.

Not only must there be a universal fight against sin; there must also be a constant fight against it. We must put sin to death continually, every day, as the flesh seeks to assert itself in various ways in our lives. No believer, regardless of how spiritually mature he or she may be, ever gets beyond the need to mortify the sinful deeds of the body. John Owen said, "Even the choicest saints who seek to remain free from the condemning power of sin need to make it their business, as long as they live, to mortify the indwelling power of sin."[3]

To mortify sin we must focus on its true nature. So often we are troubled with a persistent sin *only* because it disturbs our peace and makes us feel guilty. We need to focus on it as an act of rebellion against God. Our rebellion is of course against the sovereign authority of God. But it is also rebellion against our heavenly Father who loved us and sent His Son to die for us. God our Father is grieved by our sins. Genesis tells us that when "The LORD saw how great man's wickedness on earth had become . . . . The LORD was grieved that he had made man on the earth, and his heart was filled with pain" (Genesis 6:5-6). Your sin and my sin are not only acts of rebellion; they are acts that grieve God. And yet, He sent His Son to die for those very sins that fill His heart with pain.

The verb *mortify*, or put to death, is used eleven times in the New Testament. In nine of those instances it refers to a literal putting to death of a person. In each of those nine times there is in the context an underlying hostility, not only toward the person, but also toward what that person stood for. For example, in Matthew 10:21 the Bible tells us that "children will rebel against their parents and have them put to death." The hostility is not only toward the parents but also toward their authority. It is only authority that can be rebelled against. Several of the nine instances refer to putting Jesus to death (Matthew 26:59, 27:1). He was not put to death because of who He was but because of what He stood for. Stephen, the first Christian martyr, was put to death because of his bold, uncompromising witness for Jesus Christ (Acts 7).

Now apply that sense of hostility toward the sin you

wish to mortify. See it for what it is and for what it stands for—a rebellion against God, a breaking of His law, a despising of His authority, a grieving of His heart. This is where mortification actually begins, with a right attitude toward sin. It begins with the realization that sin is wrong, not because of what it does to me, or my spouse, or child, or neighbor, but because it is an act of rebellion against the infinitely holy and majestic God who sent His Son to be the propitiation for my sins.

Think of an unusually persistent sin in your life—perhaps some secret lust that lies in your heart that only you know about. You say you cannot overcome it. Why not? Is it because you exalt your secret desire above the will of God? If we are to succeed in putting sin to death, we must realize that the sin we are dealing with is none other than a continual exalting of our desire over God's known will.

MORTIFY YOUR SINFUL DESIRES

We must realize that in putting sin to death we are saying no to our own desires. Sin most often appeals to us through our desires, or what the older writers called our affections. Not all desires, of course, are sinful. We can desire to know God, to obey Him, and to serve Him. There are many good, positive desires.

The Scriptures, however, speak of deceitful desires (Ephesians 4:22), evil desires (James 1:14, 1 Peter 1:14), and sinful desires (1 Peter 2:11). It is evil desire that causes us to sin. All sin is desired, or perhaps the perceived benefits of the sin are desired, before it is acted upon. Satan appeals to us first of all through our desires. Eve saw "that the fruit of the tree was good for food and pleasing to the eye, and also desirable for gaining wisdom" (Genesis 3:6). Note how the concept of desire is implied in "good for food" and "pleasing to the eye," as well as explicitly mentioned in "desirable for gaining wisdom."

John Owen is once again very perceptive on this subject. He wrote,

Sin also carries on its war by entangling the affections [desires] and drawing them into an alliance against the mind [our reason]. Grace may be enthroned in the mind, but if sin controls the affections, it has seized a fort from which it will continually assault the soul. Hence, as we shall see, mortification is chiefly directed to take place upon the affections.[4]

Mortification involves a struggle between what we *know* to be right (our convictions) and what we *desire* to do. This is the struggle depicted by the Apostle Paul when he wrote, "For the sinful nature desires what is contrary to the Spirit, and the Spirit what is contrary to the sinful nature. They are in conflict with each other, so that you do not do what you want" (Galatians 5:17). The person who tends to over-indulge in sweets will struggle between a conviction about the importance of self-control and the desire to eat that delicious, tempting dessert. The man who has developed a habit of undisciplined and wandering eyes will struggle between a conviction regarding purity and the desire to indulge a lustful look. Whatever our particular areas of vulnerability to sin are, mortification is going to involve struggle—often intense struggle—in those areas.

The ceaselessness of this struggle is suggested to us in Proverbs 27:20—

Death and Destruction are never satisfied,
    and neither are the eyes of man.

Our eyes, of course, are often the gateway to our desires. But whether the appeal to our desires comes through the eye or another avenue such as the memory, our desires are never satisfied. But it is these sinful desires that must be mortified; that is, subdued and weakened in their power to entice us into sin.

It is always emotionally painful to say no to those desires, especially when they represent recurring sin patterns, because those desires run deep and strong. They cry out for fulfillment. That is why Paul used such strong language as "put to death."

TWO ARE BETTER THAN ONE

Since mortification is a difficult work, aimed at subduing strong desires and deeply ingrained habits, we need the help of one or two friends to engage in the struggle with us. These friends should be believers who share our commitment to the pursuit of holiness and who are also willing to be mutually open with us about their own struggles.

The principle underlying this aid to mortification is called synergism and is well expressed in Ecclesiastes 4:9-10—

> Two are better than one,
>> because they have a good return for their work:
> If one falls down,
>> his friend can help him up.
> But pity the man who falls
>> and has no one to help him up!

In everyday language, synergism means that two people working together can accomplish more than the same two working by themselves.

In the battle of putting sin to death, we need the mutual encouragement, challenge, and prayer support of one another. That is why spiritual synergism is so often taught in the New Testament. For example, we are to admonish one another (Colossians 3:16), encourage one another (Hebrews 3:13), confess our sins to one another (James 5:16), bear one another's burdens (Galatians 6:2), and pray for one another (James 5:16).

Although the principle of spiritual synergism applies to every aspect of the Christian life, it is certainly helpful in the pursuit of holiness. We need at least one other person of like heart to pray with us, encourage us, and if necessary, admonish us. This person (or persons) must be someone who is also involved in the struggle to mortify sin in his or her own life, so that he or she can enter into our struggles and not be scandalized by the nature of our deepest sins. It is said that the Puritans used to ask God for one "bosom friend" with whom they could share absolutely everything. This is the type of friend we should also pray for and seek out to help us in our struggle to mortify sin in our lives. Remember, however, it is a mutual effort. Each of us in a "one-another" relationship should be committed to both helping and receiving help.

MORTIFICATION AND VIVIFICATION
As we emphasize the importance of putting to death the sinful deeds of our bodies, we must not neglect to clothe ourselves with the qualities of Christlike character. Remember the scissors illustration in chapter 5? Both the blade of "putting off" (mortification) and the blade of "putting on" (clothing ourselves with Christlike character) must be working together. Each must receive equal emphasis. The old Puritan preachers used to speak not only of *mortification* (putting sin to death), but also of *vivification* (bringing to life the traits of the new person in Christ).

And just as it is "by the Spirit" that we put to death the misdeeds of the body, so it is by the Spirit that we put on the virtues of Christlike character. That is why Paul could say in Colossians 3:12-14 that *we* are to clothe ourselves with these qualities (emphasizing our responsibility), while in Galatians 5:22-23 he refers to Christian character traits as the "fruit of the Spirit" (emphasizing our dependence on the Spirit). The same Spirit who enables us to mortify sin also enables us to put on godly character.

CHOICES AND THE GRACE OF GOD
I have already addressed in chapter 8 the absolute necessity of depending on the Holy Spirit to enable us to pursue holiness. But since we have just looked at Galatians 5:17, we should direct our attention to the immediately preceding

verse, which says, "So I say, live by the Spirit, and you will not gratify the desires of the sinful nature." It is as we live by the Spirit—that is, in dependence on and obedience to Him—that we will not gratify the desires of the sinful nature.

We must realize that the Spirit's dwelling within us to instruct us and enable us is a gift of God's grace. In 2 Timothy 2:1 Paul urged Timothy to "be strong in the grace that is in Christ Jesus," but in Philippians 4:13 he spoke of "him who gives me strength." To be strong in the grace that is in Christ is to be strong in the power of the Holy Spirit, whose presence is a gift of His grace. So all that we accomplish in mortifying our sinful deeds and putting on godly character is a result of God's grace to us.

We must also realize that the discipline of mortification will be attended by a certain amount of failure. In fact, as we initially begin to mortify a particular sin, we will often fail more than we succeed. This is where we need to realize that we stand before God on the basis of His grace rather than our performance.

I realize there is a fine line between using grace as an excuse for sin and using grace as a remedy for our sin. John Owen once again had keen insight as he addressed using grace as an excuse for sin. He wrote,

> Here then is where the deceit of sin intervenes. It separates the doctrine of grace from its purpose. It persuades us to dwell upon the notion of grace and diverts our attention from the influence that grace gives to achieve its proper application in holy lives. From the doctrine of assured pardon of sin, it insinuates a carelessness for sin. . . . the soul—needing frequently to return to gospel grace because of guilt—allows grace to become commonplace and ordinary. Having found a good medicine for its wound, it then takes it for granted.[5]

The solution to staying on the right side of the fine line between using and abusing grace is repentance. The road to repentance is godly sorrow (2 Corinthians 7:10). Godly sorrow is developed when we focus on the true nature of sin as an offense against God rather than something that makes us feel guilty. Sin is an affront to God's holiness, it grieves His Holy Spirit, and it wounds afresh the Lord Jesus Christ. It also gratifies Satan, the archenemy of God. Dwelling on the true nature of sin leads us to godly sorrow, which in turn leads us to repentance.

Having come to repentance, however, we must by faith lay hold of the cleansing blood of Christ, which alone can cleanse our consciences. In fact, it is faith in Christ and the assurance of the efficacy of His cleansing blood that leads us to repentance.

David's experience is very helpful to us in the relationship of repentance and grace. David wrote,

> Blessed is he
> whose transgressions are forgiven,
> whose sins are covered.
> Blessed is the man
> whose sin the LORD does not count against him
> and in whose spirit is no deceit.
> When I kept silent,
> my bones wasted away
> through my groaning all day long.
> For day and night
> your hand was heavy upon me;
> my strength was sapped
> as in the heat of summer.
> Then I acknowledged my sin to you
> and did not cover up my iniquity.
> I said, "I will confess
> my transgressions to the LORD"—
> and you forgave
> the guilt of my sin. (Psalm 32:1-5)

David stated the conclusion first in verses 1-2, where he spoke of the blessedness of being forgiven. Then he explained why he spoke of such blessedness by acknowledging his own guilt and his miserable condition before his repentance. But with genuine repentance came the deep assurance that he was forgiven. In sequence of time, verses 1 and 2 actually come after verse 5. But as we often do, David gave the "bottom line" before explaining how he got there.

We must do as David did if we want to experience the grace of God in our failures at mortifying sin. It is not that repentance earns God's forgiveness. Only the blood of Christ does that. God, however, does deal with us as a loving but firm father deals with his children. He accepts us unconditionally because we are His sons and daughters in Christ, but He disciplines us for our good. And in the administering of His discipline He withholds the assurance of His forgiveness until we through repentance are ready to receive it.

THE MOTIVATION OF THE GOSPEL

We must, however, keep going back to His grace. Only the grace of God revealed in the gospel of Jesus Christ will give us the courage to get up again and keep on going even after we have failed for the umpteenth time. It is only grace that will allow us to be as honest about our sin as David was about his. Remember the statement that "discipline without desire is drudgery." Where will the desire to engage in the discipline of mortification come from? It will only come from the gratitude and joy of knowing that however miserably I have failed, God's grace is greater than my sin.

Over one hundred years ago the godly Scottish pastor, Horatius Bonar, wrote the following words, which are so applicable to this subject of grace and forgiveness:

It is forgiveness that sets a man working for God. He does not work in order to be forgiven, but because he has been forgiven, and the consciousness of his sin being pardoned makes him long more for its entire removal than ever he did before.

An unforgiven man cannot work. He has not the will, nor the power, nor the liberty. He is in chains. Israel in Egypt could not serve Jehovah. "Let my people go, that they may serve Me," was God's message to Pharaoh (Exod. 8:1): first liberty, then service.

A forgiven man is the true worker, the true Lawkeeper. He can, he will, he must work for God. He has come into contact with that part of God's character which warms his cold heart. Forgiving love constrains him. He cannot but work for Him who has removed his sins from him as far as the east is from the west. Forgiveness has made him a free man, and given him a new and most loving Master. Forgiveness, received freely from the God and Father of our Lord Jesus Christ, acts as a spring, an impulse, a stimulus of divine potency. It is more irresistible than law, or terror, or threat.[6]

We have all experienced the joy and motivation of this forgiveness that Bonar wrote about. But too many of us have lost sight of it and have slipped into a performance relationship with God. The only cure for this is to come back to the gospel and begin to preach it to ourselves every day. It is only the gospel that will keep us living by grace. And it is only grace that will give us the courage and motivation to mortify sin and to keep seeking to make the right choices even when we fail so often.

12

THE DISCIPLINE OF WATCHING

*"Watch and pray so that you will not fall into temptation.
The spirit is willing, but the body is weak."*
MATTHEW 26:41

ON APRIL 10, 1912, the steamship *Titanic* set sail on its maiden voyage from Southampton, England, to New York City. The largest passenger ship in the world to that time, it was also hoped to be the fastest. The captain, in an effort to break the transatlantic crossing record, had the engines going at full speed. Two days out of New York and well on its way to breaking the record, however, the *Titanic* collided with an iceberg and quickly became the world's greatest maritime disaster.

Although the collision was due to a combination of errors, the overall cause of the disaster could be summed up in a single phrase: lack of watchfulness. Despite the fact that the captain knew they were sailing directly into an area of dangerous ice packs, no special precautions were taken. Radio messages from other ships warning of ice were either taken lightly or ignored altogether. One critical message was not even copied by the wireless operator because he was too busy sending personal messages from the ship's wealthy passengers to their friends and families ashore.

The lookout in the crow's nest did not bother to report that the binoculars that might have enabled him to see the iceberg earlier were missing. Intent on breaking the speed record, the captain did not slow the ship to a more prudent speed. In short, no precautions to avoid icebergs were taken. In hindsight, such an indifferent attitude toward the single most dangerous hazard to North Atlantic shipping seems to us today to be the height of folly and irresponsibility. Yet this is the same attitude with which many believers approach the Christian life.

To use the nautical analogy, every day we sail through a sea infested with icebergs of temptation. Or to change the metaphor, every day we walk through a spiritual minefield of enemy-held territory. Despite the dangers, however, there seems to be a casual attitude toward temptation. We are either not too concerned, or else have an "it couldn't happen to me" attitude toward sin. We virtually ignore Jesus' warning to "Watch and pray so that you will not fall into temptation" (Matthew 26:41).

KNOW YOUR ENEMY

If we are going to watch against temptation, we need to be aware of its sources and behavior. To again use an analogy from warfare—and we are indeed engaged in spiritual warfare—we need some intelligence information about the enemy.

The Bible speaks of three different sources of temptation: the world, the flesh, and the Devil. Although references to and warnings about each are scattered throughout the New Testament, the one passage of Scripture that gathers all three together into one succinct statement is Ephesians 2:1-3. This passage actually speaks of our subjection to the world, the flesh (or sinful nature—see note 1, chapter 11), and the Devil before our salvation. But they still wage war against us as children of God. Therefore, we need to know how they operate and how they tempt us.

The world, or the sinful society in which we live, is characterized by the subtle and relentless pressure it brings to bear upon us to conform to its values and practices. It creeps up on us little by little. What was once unthinkable becomes thinkable, then doable, and finally acceptable to society at large. Sin becomes respectable, and so Christians finally embrace it. It is my perception that Christians are no more than five to ten years behind the world in embracing most sinful practices.

Not only is the world subtle and relentless; it is also pervasive in the pressure it brings to bear upon us. Advertising constantly holds out to us the pursuit of pleasure, possessions, and prestige as the highest good. Pop psychology promotes self-fulfillment and personal happiness—certainly not the pursuit of holiness. Magazines, movies, and television programs designed to appeal to our prurient interest find their way into our living rooms and then into our minds.

Over time the world tends to wear down our resistance to sin. Values and practices that were at one time recognized as sinful become acceptable to us simply because our otherwise nice, decent neighbors hold those values. No iceberg-infested sea was ever more dangerous than the society in which we live every day. It is the height of folly, then, *not* to watch against the temptations of the world.

The Devil, or Satan, is the god of this world and the ultimate mastermind and strategist behind all the temptations that come to us from society. Beyond that, however, he often tempts us directly. He "prowls around like a roaring lion looking for someone to devour" (1 Peter 5:8). It is difficult and perhaps unnecessary to try to distinguish between a temptation from the world and one from Satan. In general, however, temptations from the world tend to be subtle, gradual, and insidious, whereas Satan's direct attacks are more often sudden, violent, and vicious. To use a colloquial expression, Satan will attempt to "blindside" us, seeking to catch us off guard and unprepared to withstand his assaults.

Take the sin of immorality for an example. People usually slip into that over time through little indiscretions with a person of the opposite sex. The act is then fantasized in the mind before it is eventually acted out. Sometimes, however, Satan will make a bold frontal attack in that area. A Sunday school teacher was sitting alone in church one Sunday because his wife was ill. A woman from his class, who apparently had an unhappy marriage, sat down next to him and subtly began to suggest an affair. This temptation came out of nowhere without warning, in an environment where one would least expect it. This would appear to be a direct frontal assault from the Devil.

IT IS US

As dangerous as are the world and the Devil, neither is our greatest problem. Our greatest source of temptation dwells within us. It is what the Apostle Paul called the flesh, or the sinful nature. It is the principle of sin that still remains within us, even though it no longer exercises dominion. According to Sinclair Ferguson, John Owen stressed that "Freedom from the dominion of sin is not . . . the same thing as freedom from its presence and influence. Indeed, the power of sin remains where the dominion has been banished, and though that power of sin 'be *weakened*, yet its nature is not *changed*.'"[1]

As I indicated in an earlier chapter, indwelling sin now wages guerrilla warfare against us, and as any military person will attest, that is the most difficult warfare to defend against. Paul called indwelling sin a law, or as we would say, a principle, that is at work within us constantly seeking to draw us into sin (Romans 7:21-25). James referred to this principle of sin when he said, "But each one is tempted when, by his own evil desire, he is dragged away and enticed" (James 1:14). As an old Pogo cartoon years ago expressed it, "We have met the enemy and it is us."

KNOW YOURSELF

The evil desire within us constantly searches for occasions to express itself. It is like a radar system whose antenna is constantly scanning the environment for temptations to which it can respond. Some years ago, when I was continually indulging my desire for ice cream (which I don't do anymore), my eyes would automatically be drawn to a Baskin-Robbins (or any competitor brand) ice-cream store. It was uncanny. I could pass the signs of a score of stores without consciously seeing them, but I never failed to see the sign of an ice-cream store.

Recently I became interested in a certain model car. It was the same make as the one I drive, but a nicer, more expensive model. As soon as I became interested in that particular car, I noticed every one I passed on the street. I began to think of reasons why I needed that nicer model. It was roomier, more comfortable on a long trip, and had a better transmission. I finally concluded, rather reluctantly, that I really didn't need that car. But the point is, during that time my antenna was "tuned" for that model car.

Perhaps the indulgence with ice cream and the fixation on a nicer model car seem rather benign compared to temptations you've faced. You may be thinking, *Come on, let's talk about some real sins—covetousness, lust, envy, resentment, lying to customers, or cheating on exams.* Well, first of all, the indulgence in ice cream and the preoccupation with a nicer car may not be so benign, but either way, those issues demonstrate the principle: our flesh is always searching out opportunities to gratify itself according to the particular sinful desires each of us has.

STUDY YOUR WEAKNESSES
So we must study our own individual propensities to sin. Without knowledge of ourselves and our own particular weaknesses toward sin, we cannot watch against those temptations. Proverbs 27:12 says,

> The prudent see danger and take refuge,
>   but the simple keep going and suffer for it.

The captain of the *Titanic* very likely could have avoided the iceberg by applying that simple principle. In the same way, we can avoid temptations if we will simply see the obvious danger and take refuge.

Once in a hotel room alone I turned on the television to see if there was anything interesting to watch. I paused at a channel where a movie was in progress. Since I caught the show partway through, I was trying to figure out the plot. Suddenly without warning, the female main character undressed and hopped into bed with the other lead character, a man. I sat there stunned. I had heard about such movies but had never before seen one. But then, because I have a lustful heart like most men, I continued to watch to see if she would do it again.

I learned my lesson. I cannot trust myself to turn on the television when I am alone in a hotel room, unless it is to watch a specific program like the news, or a sports event, or something where I know the overall content of the program beforehand. Knowing my own lustful heart and the likelihood of seeing something on television that will play to that lust, I must, as the proverb says, "see danger and take refuge." The way I have taken refuge is to make a commitment to never turn on the television at random when I am alone in a hotel room. (Incidentally, this illustrates the type of specific commitment to which I was referring in chapter 9.)

We have already addressed the area of persistent sin patterns in our lives, those temptations to which we are especially vulnerable. We have seen that, having identified our own areas of vulnerability, we should make definite commitments regarding them, pray about them, and memorize specific verses of Scripture that will strengthen us against those temptations. Now we should add another help: Be especially watchful against them. Realize that your "temptation antenna" is constantly scanning your environment looking for those areas of sin. Then watch and pray against them.

Some of your temptations may arise from your temperament. You may be given to a quick temper, or moroseness, or laziness, or a tendency to control others. One great blessing of living by grace is that, because God no longer counts those sins against us, we can honestly face up to them and begin to mortify them with the aid of the Holy Spirit. But in order to mortify them, we must be alert for those particular sins as they seek to assert themselves.

We may be exposed to other temptations because of the occupation or profession we are in. The advertising copywriter may be under pressure to "puff" a product. The salesperson may be asked to lie. The building tradesperson may be tempted to fudge on the building code or do shoddy work in other ways. The person who has a company expense account may be tempted to cheat, and so may students in a competitive academic environment.

Each of us is exposed to a number of temptations. We should study both ourselves and our situations to identify those areas where we are, or may be, especially vulnerable, then determine how we can best guard against them.

AREAS OF STRENGTH

I was telling a friend about an adulterous affair another Christian worker had become involved in. (It was not gossip; I did not identify the person involved, and my friend would not have known him anyway.) I said to my friend, "When I learn about things like that it scares me. I think, *Could it happen to me?*" My friend responded that he was not concerned for himself because he had long ago set up certain guidelines to govern his association with women.

His self-confidence startled me. While I appreciated the guidelines he had established for himself, I could not help but think of 1 Corinthians 10:12, "So, if you think you are standing firm, be careful that you don't fall!" Remember the Sunday school teacher sitting alone in church who was approached by a lonely woman? My friend's guidelines would not have covered that situation. We can never get to the place where we don't need to watch, even in areas where we think we are strong. As John Owen said, "When [indwelling sin] is least felt, it is in fact most powerful."[2]

I attended a Prison Fellowship seminar, and one of the prisoners who gave his testimony was a former judge. My stereotype of prisoners was shattered. Here was a man who had sworn to uphold the law and administer justice, who had himself been convicted of a crime. Then I thought of David, the man after God's own heart (Acts 13:22), the man who was chosen to write most of the Psalms, one of the most beautiful and inspiring parts of all Scripture. But with all his spiritual privileges David still committed adultery and then conspired to murder to cover up his adultery. I thought to myself, *If David had committed his crime today, he would have been sent to prison.* Then I thought, *Am I stronger than David?*

I have often heard a well-known Christian teacher say, "There is no sin which I am not capable of committing." I think this teacher is much better fortified against temptation than the man who had such self-confidence regarding the sin of adultery. Our only safeguard is a sense of deep humility as we realize how powerful indwelling sin still is. Never begin to think there are areas of temptation where you don't need to be on your guard. That could be your downfall. So we need to watch in areas of known weakness because that is where we are so prone to yield to temptation. And we need to watch in areas where we think we are strong, because that is where we are apt to trust ourselves and not depend on God.

John Owen is again helpful to us in this matter.

> When we realize a constant enemy of the soul abides within us, what diligence and watchfulness we should have! How woeful is the sloth and negligence then of so many who live blind and asleep to this reality of sin. There is an exceeding efficacy and power in the indwelling sin of believers, for it constantly inclines itself towards evil. We need to be awake, then, if our hearts would know the ways of God. Our enemy is not only *upon us*, as it was with Samson, but it is also *in us*.[3]

LITTLE THINGS

Another area where we need to be watchful is the little things of everyday life, the little issues that seem so unimportant—the little lie, the little bit of pride, the little lustful glance, or the little bit of gossip. These may seem too small to bother about, but the Scripture says they are "the little foxes that ruin the vineyards" (Song of Songs 2:15).

Horatius Bonar wrote the following concerning the little things of life:

> The avoidance of little evils, little sins, little inconsistencies, little weaknesses, little follies, little indiscretions and imprudences, little foibles, little indulgences of self and of the flesh, little acts of indolence or indecision or slovenliness or cowardice, little equivocations or aberrations from high integrity, little touches of shabbiness and meanness, . . . little indifferences to the feelings or wishes of others, little outbreaks of temper, or crossness, or selfishness, or vanity—the avoidance of such *little* things as these goes far to make up at least the negative beauty of a holy life.[4]

That is a long list, but I encourage you to prayerfully read over it again to see which little things Bonar mentions may be a problem for you.

Life is largely a mosaic of little events and little deeds. It is the decision we make when the cashier at the supermarket gives us too much change, or the waiter at the restaurant understates our bill, that reveals whether we are honest or not. It may seem as if I tend to trivialize life by frequently using illustrations of sins that some consider not too big an issue. But the truth is, it is in the minutiae of life where most of us live day after day. We seldom have to say *no* to an outright temptation to adultery. We often have to say *no* to the temptation to the lustful look or thought. And as some unknown person has said, "He that despises little things shall fall little by little."

The Puritan, Thomas Brooks, wrote, "Greater sins do sooner startle the soul, and awaken and rouse up the soul to repentance, than lesser sins do. Little sins often slide into the soul, and breed, and work secretly and undiscernibly in the soul, till they come to be so strong, as to trample upon the soul, and to cut the throat of the soul."[5]

Some years ago I began to pray, "Lord, keep me on a short leash." By that I meant, don't let me get away with the little sins. Give me a tender conscience that will recognize the little sins and sound the alarm bell in my heart. Over time I'm afraid that simple prayer has been neglected, and one of my own applications from this chapter is to reinstate that request in my own prayer life. I commend it to you, also.

CHRISTIAN LIBERTY

A wealthy woman wanted to hire a chauffeur. As each applicant came to be interviewed, she had him drive her along a narrow, winding mountain road with a precipice on one side. All of the drivers, in an effort to impress her with their driving skills, drove as close to the edge of the precipice as they dared. Finally one applicant drove differently. He kept as far away from the edge as he could. The widow hired that man. She did not want a daring, albeit highly skilled, driver. She wanted one who would drive as safely as he could.

Whether that story is true or merely apocryphal, it illustrates an important principle in spiritual watchfulness. In the area of Christian liberty, our goal should be "how safe can I be" instead of "how daring can I be." Christian liberty is the term used to cover the multitude of activities where the Bible does not give us specific guidance. In those areas we have liberty or freedom to choose for ourselves what to do, subject to certain guiding principles in Scripture.

One key principle is stated in Galatians 5:13—"You, my brothers, were called to be free. But do not use your freedom to indulge the sinful nature; rather, serve one another in love." The principle is, we are not to use our liberty or freedom in Christ to indulge the sinful nature.

Actually the Apostle Paul's warning is not against indulging the sinful nature as much as it is allowing the sinful nature to use our freedom as an opportunity or occasion to assert itself. The New American Standard Bible helps us see this as it reads, "only do not turn your freedom into an opportunity for the flesh." Our flesh will actively seek to use our freedom as an opportunity or a springboard to indulge itself if we allow it to do so.

Ronald Y. K. Fung wrote, "The word rendered 'opportunity' or 'occasion' . . . is used in a military sense of a base of operations . . . ; here the imagery suggested is of the 'flesh' occupying the position of the malicious opponent and using 'freedom' as a springboard for its activities."[6] Such is the deceitful nature of our flesh. It will seek to draw us closer and closer to the precipice of sin under the guise of "asserting our freedom."

Herman Ridderbos wrote, "This freedom may not become an occasion [point of departure, bridgehead] for the flesh, that is, for sinful human nature, for wicked impulse. The flesh wants freedom to express itself as it will. Christ has not called the believers for such a freedom."[7] Turning Christian liberty into a license to sin is an evil that is ingrained in sinful human nature. It is easy to construe liberty as the right to do what one wants to do.

Knowing that our sinful human nature has this tendency, we ought to be especially watchful against it. In my younger years the Christian community attempted to do this watching for us as it came up with its various lists of "don'ts." This practice resulted in a modern Pharisaism wherein specific rules of behavior, or "sins" to avoid, were added to the Bible as God's will for us.[8]

More recently there has been a reaction against such legalism, and perhaps rightly so. But we need to be watchful that in our assertion of our freedom we do not give the flesh the opportunity to lead us over the precipice into sin. To return to the chauffeur story, do we want to see how daringly close we can come to the edge, or do we want to see how safely we can navigate the hazards of our spiritual journeys?

Scripture does say that

> The heart is deceitful above all things
> and beyond cure.
> Who can understand it? (Jeremiah 17:9)

Knowing that our hearts are deceitful by nature, we should be especially watchful that they do not turn our liberty into license. How then can we watch in this area of Christian freedom? Paul gave some specific guidelines to the Corinthian believers who were asserting their freedom in Christ. The following come from 1 Corinthians 6:12 and 10:23-24—

> "Everything is permissible for me"—but not every-thing is beneficial. "Everything is permissible for me"—but I will not be mastered by anything.

> "Everything is permissible"—but not everything is beneficial. "Everything is permissible"—but not everything is constructive. Nobody should seek his own good, but the good of others.

Commentaries on 1 Corinthians agree that "Everything is permissible for me" is almost certainly a slogan the Corinthians used to promote their idea of Christian free-dom. They used it as a rationale for driving as close to the edge of the precipice as they possibly could. They were not interested in safety from temptation but in freedom from any restraints. Paul did not deny their concept of freedom, but rather sought to point them to better principles for con-trolling the freedom he agreed they had. In response to their assertion that "everything is permissible," he stated three principles that I will frame in the form of questions:

❖ Is it beneficial? Does it promote my spiritual life?

❖ Is it a practice that over time will tend to master me? Will it stimulate a desire that will be difficult to control?

❖ Is it constructive? Will it promote the spiritual well-being of other believers if they engage in this practice that is permissible for me?

It is obvious from Paul's response to the assertion that "everything is permissible for me," that he was trying to draw the Corinthians back from the edge of the precipice to a place where they could safely live. More importantly, he was seeking to change their focus from "What freedom do I have to live as I please?" to "What will be most beneficial both for me and for my Christian brothers and sisters?"

Finally, as Paul concluded the section on Christian freedom, he gave one final overarching principle in 1 Corinthians 10:31—"So whether you eat or drink or whatever you do, do it all for the glory of God." This principle alone— doing whatever we do to the glory of God—should give us sufficient criteria for watching against abuse of our Christian liberty.

THE BEST DEFENSE

With all the enemies from the world and from Satan arrayed against us, and a guerrilla army of flesh within our own hearts, how can we effectively watch against the temptations that constantly beset us? The old adage "The best defense is a good offense" is good advice for watching against temptation. The best offense is meditation on the Word of God and prayer. It is surely no coincidence that they are the only two spiritual exercises that we are encouraged to do continually. We have already seen that we are to meditate on God's Word "day and night" (Psalm 1:2), and Paul exhorted us to "pray continually" (1 Thessalonians 5:17). We have also observed the power of the Word of God to keep us from sin when we considered Psalm 119:11—

> I have hidden your word in my heart
>   that I might not sin against you.

For every temptation that you face, there are specific passages of Scripture that address that issue. If you are not aware of some, ask your pastor or another mature Christian to help you find them. Then memorize those verses, meditate on them, and pray over them every day, asking the Holy Spirit to bring them to your mind in times of need. Ask, also, that He will strengthen your will to enable you to obey the word that He brings to your mind. Remember the continuum of influence we discussed in chapter 10. All of us are being influenced by both sinful society and the Word of God. We want to do all we can to move ourselves toward the "Word of God" end of the continuum by continually bringing it to bear upon our thinking.

Also remember that Jesus told us to watch *and* pray. We are not capable of watching by ourselves. Consider again the words of Psalm 127:1—

> Unless the LORD watches over the city,
>   the watchmen stand guard in vain.

Even with our best diligence, we need the extra dimension of the Lord watching for us.

One request in the Lord's Prayer is,

> "And lead us not into temptation,
>   but deliver us from the evil one." (Matthew 6:13)

This request actually has two parts: that we not be led into temptation, and that we be delivered from the Evil One. Since we know from James 1:13 that God does not tempt anyone, the first part must be understood as a request that God will not providentially bring us into the *way* of temptation. It is the prayer of the believer who sees his or her weaknesses and prays to not even encounter those temptations.

Of course, if we are praying not to be led into temptation, we should take steps ourselves to see that we do not *walk* into the way of temptation. Paul said in 1 Thessalonians 5:22, "Avoid every kind of evil." He exhorted the Corinthian church to "*flee* from sexual immorality" and Timothy to "*flee* the evil desires of youth" (1 Corinthians 6:18, 2 Timothy 2:22, emphasis added in both verses). Flee, of course, denotes a stronger response than avoid, but both are necessary. We can avoid certain temptations by not turning on the television or picking up certain magazines. But sometimes a temptation presents itself, and then we must flee. This is all part of watching.

The second half of the request Jesus taught us to pray is, "deliver us from the evil one," meaning, of course, Satan. We need to pray defensively against the attacks of Satan. Christ did defeat him on the cross (Colossians 2:15), and we must by faith lay hold of that victory as we pray that we will be delivered from his attacks.[9]

THINK SAFETY

I have been writing this chapter in a motel room in a city where I have been speaking at a conference. Each day I have gone for a walk and have passed a construction site where a new office building is being erected. At the entrance to the site is a large white sign with huge red letters that says, "THINK SAFETY."

The first time I saw the sign I thought, *That's a good idea. Every day the workers at that site are being reminded of the importance of safe working procedures.* Then I thought, *I wonder how many of them pay attention to the sign? Do most of them agree with the idea behind it but just go on with their usual practices, good or bad, as if the sign were not there? Does the sign do any good?* I don't know the answers to those questions. It depends partly on what safety instruction has been given and whether safety procedures are enforced.

One thing I do know, however. If those workers don't "think safety," sooner or later they will likely get hurt. Safety is something that cannot be taken for granted on a construction site. There are simply too many hazards.

The same is true in the Christian life. We need to learn to *think safety* in a spiritual sense. We are not on a "spiritual construction site." We are in a war with the world, the flesh, and the Devil. The hazards at a building site are not "out to get us." They simply exist in the nature of the work being done. But our spiritual enemies are out to get us. To *think safety* for us is to watch and pray. If we don't pay attention to that warning, we will get hurt.

The truth is, of course, we all do get "hurt" to some degree daily because we all sin every day. That is why we need to come back to the gospel of God's grace in Christ. The gospel of God's forgiveness of our sins through Christ's death frees us to face those sins honestly and bring them to the Cross and Jesus' cleansing blood. The freedom and joy that then comes from a cleansed conscience creates the desire and gives us the right motive to deal with those sins. We cannot effectively pursue holiness without going back again and again to the gospel. The gospel is the only foundation upon which we can build the disciplines necessary to pursue holiness. Grace and discipline cannot be separated.

13

THE DISCIPLINE
OF ADVERSITY

Endure hardship as discipline; God is treating you as sons.
For what son is not disciplined by his father?
HEBREWS 12:7

FOR SEVERAL CHAPTERS we have been studying the disciplines that are necessary in the pursuit of holiness. We have seen that we must behold Christ in the gospel, we must learn the proper relationship of dependence and personal discipline, we must make a commitment to holiness, and we must develop Bible-based convictions. In the everyday application of Scripture we must learn to make the right choices, to mortify sin, and to watch against temptation.

The word *must* occurs five times in the last paragraph. That's considered poor writing style, and would probably earn me an F in an English composition class. But I have deliberately repeated that word to emphasize that there are indeed certain disciplines we must (oops! I used it again) practice if we are to make progress in the pursuit of holiness. Though we are continually dependent on the enabling work of the Holy Spirit, we must fulfill our responsibilities. God does not do that for us.

There is, however, one further thing we need to do. We

should relate all these disciplines back to the grace of God so that the practice of them does not cause us to think we are in a performance relationship with Him. We need to continually remind ourselves that the performance of these disciplines does not earn us one iota of favor with God. His favor comes to us strictly through the merit of Jesus Christ. We practice these disciplines, not to earn favor with God, but because they are the means God has given to enable us to pursue holiness.

One further discipline is still absolutely necessary in the process of sanctification—the discipline of adversity or hardship. Adversity is not a discipline we undertake ourselves, but is imposed on us by God as a means of spiritual growth. As Hebrews 12:10 says, "God disciplines us for our good, that we may share in his holiness." The purpose of the discipline of adversity, then, is to make us more holy.

I have used the word *discipline* in two ways in this book. In chapter 5, where we saw that grace disciplines us, I used it to mean spiritual child-training. In later chapters I used *discipline* to indicate the spiritual training for which we ourselves are responsible. So God disciplines us, and we discipline ourselves. In Hebrews 12, the writer uses *discipline* in the sense of God's spiritual child-training. However, he uses it to refer to a specific part of the child-training— adversity. Hebrews 12:4-13 is the classic passage on this subject. For our purposes we will look at verses 5 through 11.

A WORD OF ENCOURAGEMENT

And you have forgotten that word of encouragement that addresses you as sons:
"My son, do not make light of the Lord's discipline,
and do not lose heart when he rebukes you,
because the Lord disciplines those he loves,
and he punishes everyone he accepts as a
son." (Hebrews 12:5-6)

The writer of Hebrews began his instruction and exhortation on the discipline of hardship with a word of encouragement: "And you have forgotten that *word of encouragement* that addresses you as sons" (emphasis added). To encourage someone is to seek to instill courage in that person, or to fortify the person with courage. The writer wanted to instill courage in his readers by explaining the purpose behind the adversities or hardships they were encountering. To do that he quoted Proverbs 3:11-12.

The point of the encouragement is that the Lord disciplines those He loves. It would have been an accepted fact to the first-century readers of Hebrews (and should be to us today) that discipline is not the mark of a harsh father, but rather of a father who is deeply concerned for the welfare and maturity of his children. Consequently, we should realize that God's discipline, which comes to us in the form of adversity or hardship, is an indication of His loving care, not a token of His disfavor.

In verses 5 and 6 we are warned against two opposite improper reactions to God's discipline. One is to make light of, or despise, the Lord's discipline; the other is to lose heart under it. It may be difficult for us to conceive of making light of the Lord's discipline, but one way we do this is when we count His discipline of little value—as something only to be endured rather than as something for our profit.

We also despise God's discipline of adversity when we fail to see God's hand in the hardships we encounter. Instead of acknowledging them as from God, we tend to view adversities as chance occurrences, and again, as something to be endured and passed through as quickly as possible. We do not seek God's purpose in the discipline. Instead we focus entirely on finding a way of relief.

The Scriptures tell us, however, that adversities are not chance occurrences, that they, as well as our so-called blessings, all come from the hand of God. This truth is scattered throughout the Bible, but four Old Testament scriptures will help us see the Bible's teaching:

Consider what God has done:
Who can straighten
    what he has made crooked?
When times are good, be happy;
    but when times are bad, consider:
God has made the one
    as well as the other.
Therefore, a man cannot discover
    anything about his future. (Ecclesiastes 7:13-14)

"I form the light and create darkness,
    I bring prosperity and create disaster;
    I, the LORD, do all these things." (Isaiah 45:7)

Who can speak and have it happen
    if the Lord has not decreed it?
Is it not from the mouth of the Most High
    that both calamities and good things come?
        (Lamentations 3:37-38)

When disaster comes to a city,
    has not the LORD caused it? (Amos 3:6)

Some Christians have difficulty with this truth and even deny it, because they cannot believe that a "God of love" is responsible for either the individual or public disasters that come to us.[1] But the clear testimony of Scripture stands against all our protestations. So we need to recognize the hand of God in all the adversities we encounter and not make light of His discipline.

The other improper response is to "lose heart when he rebukes you." We tend to lose heart when we think God is disciplining us out of anger instead of out of love. Hebrews 12:6, however, explicitly states that "the Lord disciplines those he loves." I acknowledge it is often difficult to sense God's love when we are undergoing His discipline, but we must by faith accept the testimony of Scripture.

The Puritan Samuel Bolton (1606–1654) wrote, "God has thoughts of love in all He does to His people. The ground of His dealings with us is love (though the occasion may be sin), the manner of His dealings is love, and the purpose of His dealings is love. He has regard, in all, to our good here, to make us partakers of His holiness, and to our glory hereafter, to make us partakers of His glory."[2]

Remember, the writer's intention was to encourage us. A good part of that encouragement must come from the realization that the hardships we encounter come from a God who is not only in sovereign control of every circumstance of our lives, but who also loves us, and who deals with us only on the basis of love. He is not only the sovereign ruler of His universe, but also our heavenly Father through the Lord Jesus Christ.

So in times of adversity, do not despise it by refusing to acknowledge God's hand in it, and do not lose heart under it by failing to see His love in it.

In addition to disciplining those He loves, the Lord also "punishes everyone he accepts as a son." Punishment may serve one of two purposes: the execution of justice or the correction of character. When a person, convicted of a crime, is sent to prison, that is punishment in the execution of justice. When a parent punishes a child, that is, or at least should be, for the correction of the child's character.

Although today we usually equate discipline with punishment, the biblical use of the word *discipline*, as we have seen, had a broader meaning. Punishment would have been one aspect of the overall program of child-training. But all of God's discipline, including punishment for disobedience that He sends to us in the form of adversity, is administered in love and for our welfare.

We know that all too often human parents do not administer punishment in love and for the child's welfare. Too often a parent will inflict punishment out of the impulse of the moment, or even out of sinful passions, because he or she has been provoked by the child. Neither justice nor correction is in view. God obviously does not have sinful passion, so we must never equate His punishment of us with the emotions we so often see in a human parent.

God does punish in the execution of justice. The Scriptures say, "God is just" (2 Thessalonians 1:6) and "'It is mine to avenge; I will repay,' says the Lord" (Romans 12:19). But as far as believers are concerned, God has executed the justice we should have received on His Son on the cross. Christ fully satisfied the justice of God and turned away His wrath from us. Therefore, God's punishment of us is always corrective, it is always administered in love and for our welfare.

In times of adversity Satan will seek to plant the thought in our minds that God is angry with us and is disciplining us out of wrath. Here is another instance when we need to preach the gospel to ourselves. It is the gospel that will reassure us that the penalty for our sins has been paid, that God's justice has been fully satisfied. It is the gospel that supplies a good part of the armor of God with which we are to stand against the accusing attacks of the Devil (see Ephesians 6:13-17).

ALL HARDSHIP IS DISCIPLINE

> Endure hardship as discipline; God is treating you as sons. For what son is not disciplined by his father? If you are not disciplined (and everyone undergoes discipline), then you are illegitimate children and not true sons. (Hebrews 12:7-8)

The writer instructed us to "endure hardship as discipline." There is no qualifying adjective. He did not say, "Endure *all* hardship"; neither did he say, "Endure *some* hardship as discipline." In the absence of a qualifying adjective, we must understand him to have meant all hardship. That is, all hardship of whatever kind has a disciplinary purpose for us. There is no such thing as pain without a purpose in the life of a believer.

This does not necessarily mean a particular hardship is related to a specific act or habit of sin in our lives. It does mean that every expression of discipline has as its intended end conformity to the likeness of Christ. It is true that we often cannot see the connection between the adversity and God's purpose. It should be enough for us, however, to know that He sees the connection and the end result He intends.

Can we tell if a particular adversity is related to some specific sin in our lives? Not with certainty, but it is my own belief that the Holy Spirit will bring such a connection to our attention if we need to know in order to deal with a particular sin. If nothing comes to mind, we can pray, asking God if there is something He wants us to consciously learn. Beyond that, however, it is vain to speculate as to why God has brought a particular hardship into our lives. Part of the sanctifying process of adversity is its mystery, that is, our inability to make any sense out of a particular hardship.

Although all pain has a purpose in the mind of God, that purpose is often—it is safe to say, *usually*—hidden from us. The Apostle Paul wrote of God's ways,

How unsearchable his judgments,
and his paths beyond tracing out. (Romans 11:33)

The Williams New Testament expresses Paul's thought in an even more forceful way: "How unsearchable His decisions, and how mysterious His methods!"[3] God's ways, being infinitely higher than our ways, will usually remain a mystery to us.

When we are unable to make any sense of our circumstances, we need to come back to the assurance in Hebrews 12:7—"God is treating you as sons." Remember, He is the one in charge of sanctification in our lives. He knows exactly what and how much adversity will develop more Christlikeness in us and He will not bring, nor allow to come into our lives, any more than is needful for His purpose.

Endure *all* hardship as discipline. I don't want to trivialize hardship, but all of us know there are varying degrees of adversity. Some is life-shattering, such as the death of a loved one or a permanently disabling injury. At the opposite end of the spectrum are situations that are really no more than temporary nuisances, such as an unexpected visitor dropping by when you are working against a tight deadline. All of these circumstances and events, whether trivial or serious, are intended by God to be means of developing more Christlike character.

It is one thing, for example, to agree that we need to develop the particular fruit of the Spirit called patience. It is quite another thing to display that fruit, and do it sincerely from the heart, in a situation where someone else is really trying our patience. God by His providence, however, continually brings us into situations requiring the exercise of obedience or the exercise of one of the traits of the fruit of the Spirit.[4] The only way Christlike character is developed is in the crucible of real-life experience. And God is the one who orchestrates and superintends those particular circumstances that each of us needs.

SUBMISSION TO DISCIPLINE

> Moreover, we have all had human fathers who disciplined us and we respected them for it. How much more should we submit to the Father of our spirits and live! (Hebrews 12:9)

In order to gain the most profit from the discipline of hardship, we need to submit to it. The writer reminds us that in the human family, the children respect the father who disciplines them. This, of course, may be difficult to see in families where the father disciplines for selfish reasons, out of anger and impatience, instead of out of love for the benefit of the child. In his analogy between human parental discipline and God's discipline, however, the writer of Hebrews assumes a more normal father model.

I was fortunate to have a dad who sought to fulfill the biblical role of a father. I knew he loved me, but I also knew he would not tolerate misbehavior. His discipline was firm but kind. He disciplined me for my good. I respected his discipline even as a child and appreciated it more after I became an adult.

The writer's point, however, is that if we respected our fathers' discipline, how much more should we submit to God's discipline. Our fathers' discipline was at best imperfect, both in motive and in application. But God's discipline is perfect, exactly suited to our needs.

How then do we submit to God's discipline? Negatively, it means that we do not become angry at God, or charge Him with injustice, when very difficult circumstances come into our lives. I was prone to write, "do not *remain* angry," instead of, "do not *become* angry at God," to allow for an initial short-term reaction toward God. But I believe even short-term anger toward God is sin for which we need to repent. Even though the anger may be an emotional response, it is still a charge of injustice against God. Surely that is sin.

It is even more serious, however, when someone allows anger toward God to continue over months or even years. Such an attitude amounts to a grudge against God and is actually rebellion. It is certainly not submitting to our heavenly Father.

Positively, we submit to God's discipline when we accept all hardship as coming from His loving hand for our good. This means that our primary response would be one of humble submission and trust. As the Apostle Peter wrote, "Humble yourselves, therefore, under God's mighty hand, that he may lift you up in due time" (1 Peter 5:6). We should submit to God's providential dealings with us, knowing that there is still much in our characters that needs improving. We should trust Him, believing that He is infinite in His wisdom and knows exactly the kind and extent of adversity we need to accomplish His purpose.

John Owen said that to submit to the Father of our spirits denotes,

> an acquiescence in His sovereign right to do what He will with us as His own; a renunciation of self-will; an acknowledgment of His righteousness and wisdom in all His dealings with us; a sense of His care and love, with a due apprehension of the end of His chastisements; a diligent application of ourselves unto His mind and will, or to what He calls us to in an especial manner at that season; a keeping of our souls by persevering faith from weariness and despondency; a full resignation of ourselves to His will, as to the matter, manner, times, and continuance of our afflictions.[5]

Owen's quote is a mouthful, but I have used it because it is such a complete description of the attitude and response toward adversity we need to develop. I encourage you to go back over it several times until you fully grasp what he said.

Submitting to God's discipline doesn't mean we should not pray for relief from the difficulty, or should not seek legitimate means to gain relief. Sometimes the end God has in mind is to exercise our faith, so He brings us into straitened circumstances so that we might look up to Him and see His deliverance. But strengthening our faith is an important aspect of discipline.

The main thing is our attitude. We can pray earnestly to God for relief and still be submissive to Him regarding the outcome. Jesus is our supreme example in this as He prayed the night before His crucifixion, "My Father, if it is possible, may this cup be taken from me. Yet not as I will, but as you will" (Matthew 26:39).

THE GOAL OF ADVERSITY

Our fathers disciplined us for a little while as they thought best; but God disciplines us for our good,

that we may share in his holiness. No discipline
seems pleasant at the time, but painful. Later on,
however, it produces a harvest of righteousness and
peace for those who have been trained by it.
(Hebrews 12:10-11)

The writer of Hebrews contrasts the finite wisdom of human
parents in disciplining children with the infinite, infallible
wisdom of God. Even the best human parents can only discipline as they *think* best. Their judgment is fallible, their
actions are sometimes inconsistent and are often guided by
the impulse of the moment. As is often observed, they have
to learn by doing. Anyone who has tried to rear children in
a godly, responsible manner knows there are times when
parents simply do not know what is the appropriate manner or degree of discipline for a child.

God, however, always disciplines us for our good. He
knows what is best for each one of us. He doesn't have to
debate with Himself over what is most suitable for us. He
knows intuitively and perfectly the nature, intensity, and
duration of adversity that will best serve His purpose to make
us partakers of His holiness. He never brings more pain than
is needed to accomplish His purpose. Lamentations 3:33
expresses that sentiment this way:

For he does not willingly bring affliction
or grief to the children of men.

Returning to Hebrews 12:10—"God disciplines us for
our good, that we may share in his holiness." Observe how
the writer equated our good with becoming more holy. The
Apostle Paul wrote in a similar manner when he said, "And
we know that in all things God works for the good of those
who love him. . . . For those God foreknew he also predestined to be conformed to the likeness of his Son" (Romans
8:28-29). To be conformed to the likeness of Christ and to
share in God's holiness are equivalent expressions. That is

the highest good to which the believer can aspire.

This is the design of God in all of the adversity and heartache we experience in this life. There is no such thing as random or chance events in our lives. All pain we experience is intended to move us closer to the goal of being holy as He is holy.

"No discipline seems pleasant at the time," the writer to the Hebrews said. Adversity comes in many forms: serious illness or injury, death of a loved one, unemployment, disappointments, and humiliations of various kinds. All of these afflictions are painful. They have to be to accomplish their intended purpose of pruning away what is unholy in our lives so that true holy character may be produced. We should admit the pain. I once knew a person who would recount some of the adversities her family was facing and would then put on a forced smile and say, "But we are victorious." She apparently thought believers should not admit pain. But the writer of Hebrews was honest. He said the discipline of hardship is painful.

Later on, however, the discipline produces a harvest of righteousness and peace. The "harvest of righteousness" is essentially equivalent to sharing in His holiness. Discipline, then, is one of the chief means God uses to make us holy. The road to holiness is paved with adversity. If we want to be holy, we must expect the discipline of God through the heartaches and disappointments He brings or allows to come into our lives.

The discipline of hardship also produces peace for those who have been trained by it. The word *trained* used here is the same one Paul used in 1 Timothy 4:7, which he borrowed from the athletic world of that day. Philip Hughes said, "When our author [of Hebrews] describes the harvest it produces as 'peaceful' the metaphor is still that of the athletic contest, for the adjective bespeaks the rest and relaxation enjoyed by the victorious contestant once the conflict is over."[6]

Hughes was speaking of the rest that comes to the

believer when we go to be with the Lord. But there is also a peace to be enjoyed in this life for those who have learned to endure adversity as the evidence of God's fatherly hand upon them to make them more holy. F. F. Bruce captured this thought well when he wrote, "The person who accepts discipline at the hand of God as something designed by his heavenly Father for his good will cease to feel resentful and rebellious; he has 'calmed and quieted' his soul [Psalm 131:2], which thus provides fertile soil for the cultivation of a righteous life, responsive to the will of God."[7]

DESTINED FOR GLORY

It is not clear whether the author of Hebrews was writing of the peace that comes with maturity in this life, as Bruce interpreted him, or the rest that comes ultimately to the believer in eternity, as Hughes understood him. The truth is, both are taught in Scripture. Concerning this life, Paul wrote that our sufferings produce perseverance, which in turn produces character (Romans 5:3-4), and James said that the testing of our faith develops perseverance, which leads to maturity (James 1:2-5).

Our ultimate hope, though, is not in maturity of character in this life, as valuable as that is, but in the *perfection* of character in eternity. The Apostle John wrote, "When he appears, we shall be like him, for we shall see him as he is" (1 John 3:2). The often-painful process of being transformed into His likeness will be over. We shall be completely conformed to the likeness of the Lord Jesus Christ.

Looking forward to that time, Paul wrote, "I consider that our present sufferings are not worth comparing with the glory that will be revealed in us" (Romans 8:18). As I think on what Paul said, I visualize in my mind a pair of old-fashioned balance scales. Paul first puts all our sufferings, all our heartaches and disappointments, all our adversities of whatever kind from whatever source onto one side of the balance scales. Of course, the scales bottom out on that side. But then he puts on the other side the glory that will be revealed in us. As we watch, the scales do not balance or even come into some degree of unbalanced equilibrium as we might expect. Instead they now completely bottom out on the side of the glory that will be revealed in us. Paul said our sufferings *are not worth comparing* with the glory we will experience in eternity.

In his second letter to the Corinthians Paul wrote,

> Therefore we do not lose heart. Though outwardly we are wasting away, yet inwardly we are being renewed day by day. For our light and momentary troubles are achieving for us an eternal glory that far outweighs them all. So we fix our eyes not on what is seen, but on what is unseen. For what is seen is temporary, but what is unseen is eternal. (2 Corinthians 4:16-18)

Here again we see the bottoming out of the scales on the side of our eternal glory that *far outweighs* our sufferings of this life.

This is not to say that our present hardships are not painful. We have already seen from Hebrews 12:11 that they are indeed painful, and we all know this to some degree from experience. Nothing I say in this chapter is intended to minimize the pain and perplexity of adversity. But we need to learn to look by faith beyond the present pain to the eternal glory that will be revealed in us. Remember, the God who disciplines us will also glorify us.

So the discipline of adversity is given to us by God as a means of our sanctification. Our role in this discipline is to respond to it, and to acquiesce to whatever God may be doing, even though a particular instance of adversity makes no sense to us. As we do this we will see in due time the fruit of the Spirit produced in our lives.

LIVE BY GRACE

Learning to live by grace instead of by performance helps us to accept the discipline of adversity. For one thing, we realize that God is not disciplining us because of our bad performance but, on the contrary, because of His love for us. We also learn to accept that whatever our situation is, it is far better than we deserve. None of us wants to receive from God what we actually deserve, for that would be only eternal punishment. So we learn not to ask, "Why did this happen to me?" (meaning, what did I do to deserve such bad treatment from God?). Finally we learn, as the Apostle Paul did with his thorn in the flesh, that God's grace is sufficient for us (2 Corinthians 12:9), however difficult and frustrating our circumstances might be. That is, God's *enabling* grace will give us the inner spiritual strength we need to bear the pain and endure the hardship, until the time when we see the harvest of righteousness and peace produced by it.

We have seen, then, that grace and discipline—both God's discipline of us and our discipline of ourselves—far from being opposed to each other, are inextricably united together in God's program of sanctification. God's discipline *is* based on grace, there is no question about that. We are the ones who have problems with the relationship of grace and discipline, and who need to work at cultivating a proper relationship.

Recall the time line in chapter 1 (page 20) that depicts our typical view that the gospel is for the unbeliever and the duty of discipleship is for the believer. Such a division often results in the practice of a performance-based acceptance with God and a self-effort approach to the pursuit of holiness.

The Bible's message, however, is that the gospel is just as necessary for the Christian as for the unbeliever. We are to base the "duty" of discipleship on the gospel, resulting in the practice of a Christ-based acceptance with God and a Spirit-energized approach to the pursuit of holiness. The so-called duty of discipleship then becomes a joy and a delight even though it requires vigorous effort. So learn to "preach the gospel to yourself" every day, and in the joy and strength of knowing your sins are forgiven and sin's dominion is broken, press on to become holy as He is holy.

NOTES

Chapter One—How Good Is Good Enough?
1. Jerry Bridges, *The Pursuit of Holiness* (Colorado Springs, CO: NavPress, 1978).
2. Jerry Bridges, *Transforming Grace* (Colorado Springs, CO: NavPress, 1991).
3. For purposes of the overall paradigm of our typical approach to the Christian life, I have used the broad concept of discipleship. In this book I will be focusing on the second subpoint, the pursuit of holiness. For an excellent treatment of the disciplines, I recommend Donald Whitney's book, *Spiritual Disciplines for the Christian Life* (Colorado Springs, CO: NavPress, 1991).
4. Kenneth S. Wuest, *The New Testament, An Expanded Translation* (Grand Rapids, MI: Eerdmans, 1961), page 424.
5. Quoted by permission from Mutua Mahiaini.

Chapter Two—The Pharisee and the Tax Collector
1. Timothy George, *Faithful Witness—The Life and Mission of William Carey* (Birmingham, AL: New Hope, 1991), page 155.
2. This book is addressed primarily to the committed Christian. I am aware that a vast number of professing Christians display little or no commitment to spiritual growth or discipleship, and for them the Christian life is no more than the mere formalities of attending church and avoiding scandalous behavior. These people need a different message than the one in this book.
3. The primary Scripture references from which I compiled my list were Galatians 5:22-23; Ephesians 4:1-2,25-32; Colossians 3:12-17; 1 Timothy 6:6-11; James 3:17. The twenty-seven traits I found are compassion, considerateness, contentment, faith, faithfulness, forbearance, forgiving spirit, generosity, gentleness, godliness, goodness, honesty, humility, impartiality, joy, kindness, love, mercy, patience, peace, perseverance, purity, righteousness, self-control, sincerity, submissiveness, thankfulness. I undoubtedly overlooked other positive traits.
4. These action statements first appeared in my book *The Practice of Godliness* (Colorado Springs, CO: NavPress, 1983), pages 247-248.
5. J. Knox Chamblin, *Paul and the Self* (Grand Rapids, MI: Baker, 1993), pages 11-12.
6. John Owen, *Communion with God*, ed. R. J. K. Law (Edinburgh, Scotland: The Banner of Truth Trust, 1991), page 117.

Chapter Three—Preach the Gospel to Yourself

1. Reported by R. C. Sproul in a message entitled "The Priority of Righteousness," given at Independent Presbyterian Church, Memphis, TN, September 18, 1993.
2. George Smeaton, *The Apostle's Doctrine of the Atonement* (Edinburgh, Scotland: The Banner of Truth Trust, 1991; originally published 1870), page 117. I am indebted to Dr. Smeaton for his very helpful exposition of the atonement and have used some of his ideas elsewhere in this chapter without always identifying specific phrases as direct quotations.
3. Robert Haldane, *Exposition of the Epistle to the Romans* (London: The Banner of Truth Trust, 1958; originally published ca. 1842), page 132.
4. The concept of the believer's union with Christ, both as to its meaning and its effect on the believer, will be developed in the next chapter.
5. Charles Hodge, *Commentary on the Epistle to the Romans* (Grand Rapids, MI: Eerdmans, reprint 1955; 1886), page 91.
6. D. M. Lloyd-Jones, *Romans: An Exposition of Chapters 3:20–4:25, Atonement and Justification* (Edinburgh, Scotland: The Banner of Truth Trust, 1970), pages 75-76.
7. From the hymn "Nothing but the Blood," by Robert Lowry (1826–1899), appearing in most evangelical hymnals.

Chapter Four—We Died to Sin

1. Sinclair B. Ferguson, *The Christian Life: A Doctrinal Introduction* (Edinburgh, Scotland: The Banner of Truth Trust, 1989), page 104.
2. John Stott, *Life in Christ* (Wheaton, IL: Tyndale, 1991), page 38. Union with Christ was also taught by Jesus Himself in the vine-and-branches analogy, John 15:1-8, and by the apostles Peter and John. See 2 Peter 1:4 and 1 John 2:5-6, 3:6.
3. Sinclair Ferguson, in his chapter on "Union with Christ" in *The Christian Life*, lists six different "categories" of our union with Christ. These are indeed very helpful ways of viewing our union with Him, but all of them can be fitted into, or made to coordinate with, the traditional aspects of federal union and vital union.
4. George Smeaton, *The Apostle's Doctrine of the Atonement* (Edinburgh, Scotland: The Banner of Truth Trust, 1991; originally published 1870), page 162.
5. Smeaton, page 162.
6. Sinclair B. Ferguson, *John Owen on the Christian Life* (Edinburgh, Scotland: The Banner of Truth Trust, 1987), page 125, emphasis in original.
7. John Murray, *The Epistle to the Romans,* New International Commentary on the New Testament series (Grand Rapids, MI: Eerdmans, 1968), vol. 1, page 213.
8. For those whose high school grammar may be a bit rusty, the indicative mood of a verb is used to state a fact such as, "The dog sat." The imperative mood is used to give a command such as, "Bowser, sit."

It is also used to give an exhortation, or even to make a request.
9. Murray, page 227.

Chapter Five—Disciplined by Grace
 1. Matthew Henry, *A Commentary on the Whole Bible* (Old Tappan, NJ: Revell, n.d.), vol. 6, page 867.
 2. John Calvin, *Calvin's New Testament Commentaries*, vol. 10, *The Second Epistle of Paul to the Corinthians, and the Epistles to Timothy, Titus and Philemon*, ed. David W. Torrence and Thomas F. Torrance, trans. T. A. Smail (Grand Rapids, MI: Eerdmans, 1964), page 371.
 3. William Hendricksen, *Commentary on I and II Timothy and Titus* (London: The Banner of Truth Trust, 1959), page 370.

Chapter Six—Transformed into His Likeness
 1. Matthew Henry, *A Commentary on the Whole Bible* (Old Tappan, NJ: Revell, n.d.), vol. 4, page 962.
 2. William S. Plumer, *The Grace of Christ, or Sinners Saved by Unmerited Kindness* (Keyser, WV: Odom Publications, n.d.; originally published 1853), page 278, emphasis in original.
 3. Plumer, page 279.
 4. For a more detailed discussion of this second meaning of grace, see Jerry Bridges, *Transforming Grace* (Colorado Springs, CO: NavPress, 1991), pages 137-138.
 5. The *New International Version* says in Psalm 40:8, "I desire to do your will, O my God." All other versions at my disposal translate it, "I *delight* to do your will." See KJV, NKJV, RSV, NASB, MLB, TLB, and the *American Standard Version*.
 6. Charles Hodge, *Second Epistle to the Corinthians*, rev. ed. (London: The Banner of Truth Trust, 1959), page 78.
 7. John Murray, *Redemption—Accomplished and Applied* (London: The Banner of Truth Trust, 1961; originally published 1955), pages 144-145.
 8. Murray, page 145.
 9. Samuel Bolton, *The True Bounds of Christian Freedom* (Edinburgh, Scotland: The Banner of Truth Trust, 1964; originally published 1645), page 26.
10. Murray, page 146.
11. Murray, page 147.
12. I have used the NASB translation for 2 Corinthians 3:18, because it, as well as most other versions, says "beholding" the glory of the Lord, whereas the NIV says "reflect" the Lord's glory. Although both meanings are feasible, I believe the context favors the use of "beholding."
13. James Fraser, *A Treatise on Sanctification* (Audubon, NJ: Old Paths Publications, 1992; originally published 1774, revised 1897), pages 464-465.
14. Robert Haldane, *Exposition of the Epistle to the Romans* (London: The Banner of Truth Trust, 1958; originally published ca. 1842), pages 253-254.

Chapter Seven—Obeying the Great Commandment

1. John Calvin, *Calvin's New Testament Commentaries*, vol. 3, *A Harmony of the Gospels Matthew, Mark and Luke and the Epistles of James and Jude*, ed. David W. Torrence and Thomas F. Torrance, trans. A. W. Morrison (Grand Rapids, MI: Eerdmans, 1972), page 36.
2. Charles Hodge, *Commentary on the Epistle to the Romans* (Grand Rapids, MI: Eerdmans, reprint, 1955; 1886), page 290.
3. James Fraser, *A Treatise on Sanctification* (Audubon, NJ: Old Paths Publications, 1992; originally published 1774, revised 1897), page 418.
4. Fraser, page 418.
5. John Owen, *Communion with God*, ed. R. J. K. Law (Edinburgh, Scotland: The Banner of Truth Trust, 1991), page 13.

Chapter Eight—Dependent Discipline

1. I understand the U.S. Air Force does have one plane that is designed to fly with one engine and *part* of a wing missing.
2. F. F. Bruce, *The Epistles to the Colossians to Philemon and to the Ephesians*, New International Commentary on the New Testament series (Grand Rapids, MI: Eerdmans, 1984), page 88.
3. Paraphrased from John Owen, *The Works of John Owen*, ed. William H. Goold (Edinburgh, Scotland: The Banner of Truth Trust, 1965; originally published 1850–1853), vol. 3, page 384.
4. Paraphrased from Owen, page 529.
5. Jonathan Edwards, *The Works of Jonathan Edwards*, ed. Edward Hickman (Edinburgh, Scotland: The Banner of Truth Trust, 1974; originally published 1834), vol. 1, page xx.
6. John Murray, *The Epistle to the Romans*, New International Commentary on the New Testament series (Grand Rapids, MI: Eerdmans, 1968), vol. 1, page 294.

Chapter Nine—The Discipline of Commitment

1. Paraphrased from Frederick William Faber, *Growth in Holiness* (Westminster, MD: The Newman Press, 1960; originally published 1854), page 93.
2. Stephen Charnock, as quoted by C. H. Spurgeon in *The Treasury of David*, vol. 2, *Psalms 119–127* (Grand Rapids, MI: Baker, reprint, 1984; 1882–1887), page 249.
3. Jonathan Edwards, *The Works of Jonathan Edwards*, ed. Edward Hickman (Edinburgh, Scotland: The Banner of Truth Trust, 1974; originally published 1834), vol. 1, page xxi.
4. William Law, *A Serious Call to a Devout and Holy Life*, rev. ed. (Grand Rapids, MI: Sovereign Grace Publishers, 1971), page 6.
5. Law, pages 6, 9.
6. Law, page 7.
7. John Calvin, *Calvin's New Testament Commentaries*, vol. 8, *The Epistle of Paul to the Romans and to the Thessalonians*, ed. David W. Torrence and Thomas F. Torrance, trans. Ross Mackenzie (Grand Rapids, MI: Eerdmans, 1964), page 263.

Chapter Ten—The Discipline of Convictions
1. James Patterson and Peter Kim, *The Day America Told the Truth* (New York: Prentice-Hall, 1991), page 25.
2. Reported in *National and International Religion Report*, vol. 8, no. 5, February 21, 1994, page 2.
3. John Murray, *The Epistle to the Romans*, New International Commentary on the New Testament series (Grand Rapids, MI: Eerdmans, 1968), vol. 2, page 114.
4. John Brown, *Analytical Exposition of the Epistle of Paul to the Romans* (Grand Rapids, MI: Baker, reprint, 1981; 1857), page 437.
5. The Navigators have emphasized Scripture memorization for over sixty years. Their *Topical Memory System*, which teaches principles of memorization and provides sixty key verses of Scripture to memorize, is available from NavPress and may be purchased through your local Christian bookstore. If you have never developed the discipline of Scripture memorization, I highly recommend this program.

Chapter Eleven—The Discipline of Choices
1. The Greek word translated as "sinful nature" in the NIV literally means "flesh." Today we use the word *flesh* to refer to the soft tissue of our physical bodies. The Apostle Paul used it to refer to the sin principle that continues to dwell within us, even though we have been freed from sin's dominion. I prefer the word *flesh* instead of *sinful nature*, because the latter term can imply that the believer has two natures: a sinful and a new nature. We have one nature indwelt and spiritually animated by the Holy Spirit, but also handicapped by sin that continues to dwell within us.
2. John Owen, *Sin and Temptation*, ed. James M. Houston (Portland, OR: Multnomah, 1983), page 153.
3. Owen, page 152.
4. Owen, page 28.
5. Owen, pages 41-42.
6. Horatius Bonar, *God's Way of Holiness* (Durham, England: Evangelical Press, 1979; originally published 1864), pages 51-52.

Chapter Twelve—The Discipline of Watching
1. Sinclair B. Ferguson, *John Owen on the Christian Life* (Edinburgh, Scotland: The Banner of Truth Trust, 1987), pages 130-131, emphasis in original.
2. John Owen, *Sin and Temptation*, ed. James M. Houston (Portland, OR: Multnomah, 1983), page 5.
3. Owen, page 7, emphasis in original.
4. Horatius Bonar, *God's Way of Holiness* (Durham, England: Evangelical Press, 1979; originally published 1864), pages 109-110, emphasis in original.
5. Thomas Brooks, *The Works of Thomas Brooks* (Edinburgh, Scotland: The Banner of Truth Trust, reprint, 1980; 1861–1867), vol. 1, page 21.
6. Ronald Y. K. Fung, *The Epistle to the Galatians*, New International

Commentary on the New Testament series (Grand Rapids, MI: Eerdmans, 1988), page 244.

7. Herman N. Ridderbos, *The Epistle of Paul to the Churches of Galatia*, New International Commentary on the New Testament series (Grand Rapids MI: Eerdmans, 1953), page 200. Fung's commentary has replaced Ridderbos' in the NICNT series.

8. I address this form of legalism in chapter 9 of *Transforming Grace* (Colorado Springs, CO: NavPress, 1991).

9. Scripture indicates that God at times does allow Satan to tempt us, as he did Peter (Luke 22:31-32), but at least in that instance God was apparently using Satan to get at Peter's pride (see verse 33).

Chapter Thirteen—The Discipline of Adversity

1. I have treated this subject extensively in my book *Trusting God: Even When Life Hurts* (Colorado Springs, CO: NavPress, 1988).

2. Samuel Bolton, *The True Bounds of Christian Freedom*, rev. ed. (Edinburgh, Scotland: The Banner of Truth Trust, 1964; originally published 1645), page 25.

3. Charles B. Williams, *The New Testament in the Language of the People* (Nashville, TN: Holman Bible Publishers, 1986), page 351.

4. For those unfamiliar with the expression "the providence of God," I defined it on page 25 of my book *Trusting God: Even When Life Hurts* as, "His constant care for and His absolute rule over all His creation for His own glory and the good of His people."

5. John Owen, as quoted by John Brown in *An Exposition of Hebrews* (Edinburgh, Scotland: The Banner of Truth Trust, reprint, 1961; 1862), page 626.

6. Philip Edgecumbe Hughes, *A Commentary on the Epistle to the Hebrews* (Grand Rapids, MI: Eerdmans, 1977), pages 532-533.

7. F. F. Bruce, *The Epistle to the Hebrews*, rev. ed., New International Commentary on the New Testament series (Grand Rapids, MI: Eerdmans, 1990), page 346.

AUTHOR

JERRY BRIDGES, formerly Vice President for Corporate Affairs of The Navigators, is now a staff member with The Navigators Community Ministries Group, where he is engaged primarily in a Bible teaching ministry.

He grew up in Tyler, Texas, and is a graduate of the University of Oklahoma. While serving as an officer in the United States Navy, Jerry came in contact with The Navigators and soon felt God's call on his life to that ministry. He has served on The Navigators' staff since 1955.

Jerry is also the author of *The Pursuit of Holiness*, *The Practice of Godliness*, *Trusting God*, and *Transforming Grace*. Companion study guides are available for each of these books.

Jerry and his wife, Jane, live in Colorado Springs.